The Learning Organiza

Bob Garratt is an international management consultant who specializes in the development of directors, the strategic positioning of organizations, and cross-cultural issues. He worked at the Architectural Association School in London as administrator, lecturer in management and designer of live-project educational processes. He worked in central France on community development, then at Ulster College, Belfast, on management and community education. In 1974 he joined the team designing and running the GEC Developing Senior Managers Programme and started the transition from design to management. He has worked in many European countries, the USA, Nigeria, Bahrain, Malaysia and, since 1976, China and Hong Kong in both of which he has helped to develop management education. He designed and helped produce the TV South series *In the Mouth of the Dragon* on Hong Kong, China and Britain and has published two books: with John Stopford *Breaking Down Barriers: Priorities and Practice in International Management Education*; and with Sally Garratt *China Business Briefing*.

He is developing interactive videodisc as a management training medium, and is working on processes devoted to the development of potential directors with a group of colleagues under the banner of Metapreneur Ltd. He is an Executive Committee member of the International Foundation for Action Learning; and is Honorary Secretary of the Association for Management Education and Development. He is based in London.

Other titles for The Successful Manager

Bob Garratt

The Learning Organization

and the need for directors who think

Fontana/Collins

First published in 1987 by Fontana Paperbacks
8 Grafton Street, London W1X 3LA

Copyright © Bob Garratt 1987

Set in 10 on 12 Linotron Times
by The Word Factory Ltd, Rossendale, Lancashire
Made and printed in Great Britain by
William Collins Sons & Co. Ltd, Glasgow

Acknowledgements are made to William Heinemann
for permission to print the chart on p. 110

Conditions of Sale
This book is sold subject to the condition
that it shall not, by way of trade or otherwise,
be lent, re-sold, hired out or otherwise circulated
without the publisher's prior consent in any form of
binding or cover other than that in which it is
published and without a similar condition
including this condition being imposed
on the subsequent purchaser

To Michael Lloyd, Alvin Boyarsky and Reg Revans –

the three people who delegated the responsibility for
me to make the mistakes necessary to learn

and to the friend and tutor who kept me at it when the
distractions were many – Beverly Bernstein

Contents

PART TWO   EXPERIMENTS AND ACTION

Section One   HOW DO WE GET THERE?   85

Section Two   SOME POSSIBLE CONSEQUENCES   132

Preface

This book is designed as a keystone in the Fontana Successful Manager series. The genesis of the series was during discussions with Roger Graef and Helen Fraser of Collins about my conviction that the economic depression in the United Kingdom had created significantly different ways of thinking about managers and management than anything seen in the previous two decades. The crisis had been sufficiently large to trigger a process of reframing the social, economic, and political contexts in which management and management education are viewed.

Labour forces had been, to use the awful euphemism, 'slimmed down'. Less well known was that a similar process had occurred at director level, and is now happening with that last outpost of overmanning – the middle managers. I described to Roger Graef and Helen Fraser a phenomenon that I saw regularly at international conferences where papers were given by charismatic US academics, mid-European intellectuals, flamboyant Latins, and ever-smiling Japanese. The focus was inevitably on 'what ought to be' in management once the global shake-out was over. Theories on the need to be more lean, more concerned with product design, more responsive to the market, more competent at using the talents of the workforce, more conscious of the environment and, most of all, more skilled at learning-whilst-doing – all these were propounded. During questions, one or more bemused 'Brits' would stand up and say that they thought they had understood what had been said, and they would just like to say that they were already doing this – and that it seemed to work.

The result was electrifying and during the next break the speaker would be surrounded by enthusiastic seekers after ideas and practice. British pragmatism when faced with a crisis, plus a chronic unwillingness to codify and diffuse ideas, has led to the intriguing position that Britain currently has a repository of state-of-the-art ideas and processes for developing people and their organizations, but little way of communicating these. From this observation the idea of the Fontana Successful Manager series was developed. Practitioners were finding it necessary to redraw the field of management studies because its confines had been drawn too tightly in the past. Hopefully the series will help do that.

Central to the new ideas – it is too grand to call it a 'British school' – is the notion that learning has become the key developable and tradeable commodity of an organization. Generating and selling know-how and know-why, the learning of the organization and its people, is becoming the core of any organization which has a chance of surviving in the longer term. We already know a lot about organizational learning processes. When this is added to the new ideas on the generation of vision, the refinement of thinking processes, the development of policy and strategy, the notion of managing as a 'holistic' process, and the acquisition of new managerial skills from outside the traditional boundaries, then there is a powerful mix available.

However, there seemed to be no easily available ideas and practice to help managers design and build a workable learning organization which integrated the aspects mentioned above, and which incorporated the crucial leadership roles of the directors. Hence the writing of this book.

It is not a pure research study. It cannot be. The insights were gained initially from observations of personal development projects for managers thought to have 'director potential'. These were recorded and measured in various ways, both psychologically and personally. In all I have worked with some 1,500 top managers around the world, 300 of them in great depth and over periods of at least one year.

As this work progressed I was aware increasingly of the lack of integration of personal development activities with the development of appropriate organizational structures and processes. Why should this be so? It struck me then that the existing directors tended not to have ways of talking about these topics. They were beyond their existing vocabulary. Moreover, even the more fluent ones seemed to have little constructive idea about the role of the director in an organization. This intrigued me.

The idea that without such models and processes directors tend to be directionless is usually only talked about privately, between consenting adults. It has an aura similar to the Victorian approach to sex – it is not nice to talk about it in public. The result has been the creation of a mythology about what happens at the top of organizations – an area in which strange, sometimes exhilarating, but ultimately tragic things occur. My work showed that a great deal of such received wisdom seemed to be true. My interest was to uncover the truth of what happens and to expose it to the light of public debate in as constructive a way as I knew how. Consequently, this book is derived from some twelve years' worth of private conversations with directors and director-potential managers, and from being asked by companies to help them address the issue of how to develop their existing and new generations of directors and general managers. The book is a reflection on those twelve years.

I have used Kolb's learning cycle to give the book its structure. Part 1 is based on Reflections and Abstractions, where I have tried to stand back and reconsider what I have been viewing whilst hopefully giving it a sounder conceptual base. Part 2 deals with Experiments and Action, where I try to suggest ways in which existing and new tools may be applied to the strategic problems outlined in Part 1. During this I have kept in mind that for learning to occur it is necessary to have all four aspects of the learning cycle in operation – a matter which I argue later many directors tend to forget.

I have found both clients and programme participants to be highly supportive during my researches. They took high risks letting an outsider loose amongst their most precious resources. For their confidence in me and my ideas, and for their encouragement to raise the issues before a wider public, I shall always be grateful. In particular I would like to thank the General Electric Company, TSB Group, CASE Communications, the Plessey Company, Phicom, Ellerman Lines Ltd, The European Space Agency, the EEC Esprit Programme, ICI, Interdean, Medtronic Europe, Bank of America International, Swiss-

Nigerian Chemical Company, Aluminium Bahrain, Hutchinson Whampoa, the Hong Kong and Shanghai Bank, the Management Development Centre of Hong Kong, particularly Bob Tricker, and the State Economic Commission in Beijing, particularly Vice-Chairman Zhang Yannin and Professor Pan Chenglieh, for allowing access over the years to their top and 'fast track' managers.

Many people have supported me in my endeavour and encouraged me to record the outcome. The original group who pulled me away from design and into management have to take some responsibility for the consequences – Reg Revans, Mike Bett, David Pearce, Jean Lawrence, Tony Eccles, David Casey, and David Sutton who launched the GEC Developing Senior Managers Programme.[1] Later additions were Geoff Gaines, John Shrigley, and Hugh Allen, all of whom provided strong criticism and healthy debate. Individual insight was given by Mike Farebrother of Chloride, Bob Scott of MEL, Peter Burton, Derek Laval, and Maureen Greaves of CASE in the UK and US, Barry Welch of TSB Group, Ezra Kogan and Dave Francis through our work in Plessey, Don Young of Thorn-EMI, Mick Crews of Ellerman Lines, Mike Blakstad of BBC TV's *The Risk Business*, Jan Parsson and Roger Cunliffe of Nordic Ventures, Don Evans of Marconi Underwater Systems, Chris Lorenz of the *Financial Times*, Brian Lund of the Open Business School, Desmond McAllister of ITT, John Pontin of the JT Group, Peter Barrett of the Hong Kong Telephone Company, Rosalie Vicars-Harris and Malcolm Lewis of Media Projects International, and Fred Kohler of Learning Leaders.

The more strategic notions were scrutinized and criticized by Harold Kelner and Peter Bracken, and Rolf Hickmann and Gunnar Walstam of Procede, whilst academic help was given by Tom Lupton, John Morris, and Tudor Rickards of the Manchester Business School and, although they may not be conscious of it, the 'inner circle' I held in my head – perched like parrots on my shoulder during the writing asking discriminating questions about the validity of my scribbling – Max Boisot, Gordon Redding, Alistair Mant, John Stopford, Charles Handy, Gerry Johnson, David Steel, Ronnie Lessem, Ivor Delafield, Roger Plant, Barry Paterson, Jerry Rhodes, Sue Thame, Geert Hofstede, Jim Wilk, and Ian Cunningham.

Last, but by no means least, I must thank Sally, my wife, for letting me ruin our holiday by writing, and for her showing me how to work the word processor. Greater love than this hath . . . etc.

The resulting book is entirely my responsibility. I hope it is a credit to the many better minds than mine who have tried to give me direction.

Bob Garratt

Villa Gabrielle
Tourrettes-sur-Loup
France

May 1986

Introduction

This book argues that organizations can only become effective if the people selected to run them are capable of two key skills – learning continuously, and giving direction. The former will be dealt with in some detail in Part 2 of this book. Part 1 looks at an organizational curiosity – that most of the people at the top of organizations have not been trained in, and are uncomfortable with, giving direction to their organization. Yet that is why they are called 'directors'. Little attention is given in organizations to the induction, generation of competence in, or development of, these key people. A consequence is that directors are rarely comfortable in their jobs and seldom exercise fully the powers they have. There are two frequent effects on the organization of such uncertainty. First, a vacuum is often created at the top so that the business becomes unguided and then fragments into warring specialist factions. Second, the directors do not enjoy their exposed positions and try to seek comfort through regression – by slipping back unofficially into their old jobs, whilst keeping their new job titles and benefits.

This search for comfort rather than performance has two powerful consequences. On the one hand, it blocks the development of those promoted to take over the job previously held by the director. This has a knock-on, cascading effect down the organization which is so common in organizations around the world that one regularly finds people admitting they are paid one or two levels above the jobs they actually do. On the other hand, the search for comfort means that directors do not fulfil the basis of their organizational role. They do not give direction, do not monitor changes in the social, economic, and political environments in which they exist, and so do not ensure the survival of their organizations by being able to adapt their organizations to the rate of change in those environments.

These two consequences seem to run in parallel. The workforce and managers are frustrated at not being able to do their work properly because someone above them is trying to do it for them, and little attention is paid to external environmental changes by the directors 'because we are too busy dealing with day-to-day matters to worry about the future'. It is a formula for short-term organizational inefficiency and long-term organizational ineffectiveness. The internal and external development processes of the organization are blocked. The chances of medium- to long-term survival are decreased dramatically. It is not just a British phenomenon. The problem, and consequences, are worldwide.

What interests me particularly are the models and processes used by directors who have overcome such behaviour. This book looks at experiences of success, and disaster, and strives to develop the idea of successful organizations as primarily 'learning systems' guided by properly trained direction-givers.

A thoughtful person might ask, 'Why is this necessary? Surely all organizations must learn or they die?' This is correct. But organizations tend to take a long time to die. The time lapse between their cutting off sources of environmental information about change and their organizational death is usually measured in years, sometimes decades. There is an inertia in most organizations which outside observers find hard to credit. The organizational 'brain' may have been clinically dead for some time, but the organizational life-support machine is often kept on for years before someone finally throws the switch.

I have been working on this book for some ten years. Coming from a background which included design and the humanities, I found very odd the scientific/technical and highly convergent thinking regularly deployed by managers. I had a liberal education which started with valuing ideas and divergent thoughts, then sought to give rigour to them by making connections between the ideas and problems, derived appropriate information from a sea of data, and then used the energies present in the ambiguities and uncertainties of those problems to find elegant solutions. On entering the industrial world I found to my surprise that most managers did not think in this way, nor strive for such values. They had typically a high need for certainty, and an impulsion to action rather than thought. It was judged better to be seen doing anything rather than thinking. This need for certainty-through-doing often led only to action-fixated behaviour rather than anything likely to allow learning.

Indeed there was often resistance both to taking time to think – 'because you're paid to do things around here' – and to consciously learning because it did not feel quite 'right' managerially to admit, even to colleagues, that, as a director, one was not omniscient. In the groups with which I worked there was a constant feeling of vulnerability because they did not understand the specialist language and disciplines of the other directors, who in turn did not seem to value theirs. The idea of a director having to manage the boundaries between specialisms was, therefore, daunting. The idea of having to rise above a personal specialism to take a generalist view of the organization and its place in a changing world was considered an ideal, but beyond the job of a 'normal' director. There was little awareness of, or interest in, the outside world and its impact on the contexts in which such folk made their managerial decisions. Politics and international affairs were considered far beyond the bounds of directors and somehow 'not our concern'.

The application of the new 'hard' managerial knowledge generated during the fifties and sixties in the quantitative and analytical areas was being applied strongly in organizations in the mid-seventies. To an outsider coming newly on to the scene full of intelligent naivety it was patently not helping policy formulation, or strategic development. It was necessary but by no means sufficient to guarantee the survival of a business. Other aspects of attitude, knowledge, and skill seemed necessary to refine the role and learning processes to ensure competent directors.

It struck me then, and does now, that the selection processes of managerial talent are geared to the identification of single-function specialists only. This works well in the early stages of a manager's career. But as soon as he or she reached levels where it was necessary to integrate specialist areas, to become more generalist and to focus on the contexts in which managerial decisions of a strategic nature are made, things seemed to go awry – often dramatically so. The thinking processes and skills needed to take a wider view were not only missing but were often actively resisted by many of the directors with whom I worked. A substantial part of their broader education seemed to be missing. They appeared educationally and culturally deprived, particularly at the top organizational levels. Yet this is where it is essential to use the design processes of thought, vision, context, and integration to ensure survival and growth. I knew that this was an area where a lot could be done to help by using a wider range of disciplines than that usually considered part of 'management studies'. How to demonstrate this was another matter as the opposition seemed formidable.

The incident which triggered my interest and set me working on the idea of integrating the many cultures and disciplines which might comprise future managerial life occurred in 1975. I had been working on live-project education for senior managers in a major electronics group. One project concerned the development of a new telecommunications technology which integrated telephones with computing. It was agreed by all concerned that on this product the future of the British telecommunications industry hung. As the project developed, it became obvious that the top managers involved were thinking mainly along the lines of telephone technology, with the computing side as a bolt-on to the end of the process. The younger senior managers working on the project, already identified as potential top managers, started sending out messages that this seemed a fundamentally flawed way of thinking. They saw the telephone side as the 'easy' part of the new technology. The difficult bit was the computing integration of the system. This they identified as the enabling technology for the whole system. And it was the one in which they were weak.

Moreover, they said, if we follow this line of thinking we will be competing directly with the big computing manufacturers who, by definition, will have the key expertise already and will be able to buy the necessary telephone expertise quite cheaply from many sources. Should we not reconsider our strategy and link up with a major computer manufacturer so that we both might gain?

The matter was eventually brought up in a major meeting and the chief executive responsible for the product became very angry and eventually started to attack the project participants 'for thinking'. To be precise, he said: 'I do not pay my managers to think, but to do. If they are going to think, then they will do it in their own time – on a Sunday.' This was received in shocked silence and led to a severe drop in commitment and morale. Over the next two years the brighter and more committed managers moved out into more sympathetic projects. The work continued along the predetermined lines but the political and international contexts were changing rapidly. Top managers moved on regularly and enthusiasm waned. It was decided not to revamp the project despite increasing warnings of major environmental changes – their monopoly client was being deregulated by the government and was making ominous noises about wanting to introduce foreign competition into their purchasing policies; and marketing reports said that what was being developed was too expensively gold-plated for the export markets which had been anticipated when the initial design was drawn up.

Today this project languishes in the commercial doldrums. The hard and soft facts about it were known ten years ago but there were two fundamental problems which were not addressed by the top managers. First, there were within that business no mechanisms for openly debating and refining policy and strategy on the project, nor were there any mechanisms for integrating feedback from both the project and, simultaneously, the outside world and its changing values and demands. The top managers had set up a brainless organization, an unthinking machine, which was doomed to a long and painful organizational death as it became estranged from its environment and the knowledge, good will, and commitment of its workforce. The organization could not learn.

Second, the top managers had never taken on their true 'directing' roles in the business. They acted as the senior functional specialists of their respective disciplines and fought amongst themselves for the supremacy of that discipline over the others. They did not understand that co-operation rather than conflict is essential at the top of a business to ensure its survival. The idea that they had a final career step to take – from the comfort of their previous discipline to exposure to an environment where it was essential to integrate disciplines and resources to cope with an increasingly competitive world – was not within their thinking or aspirations. If anything, it was diametrically opposed to it. They honestly believed that if they built a technologically superior product then the world would beat a path to their door. They saw building the best mousetrap as the extent of their role as directors.

I knew back in 1975 that there were many ideas, processes, and techniques which could be applied to sort out such organizational messes, through breaking open the fettered thinking of the top technical specialists. Moreover, this seemed to offer the possibility of creating more humane organizations in the process.

This book is a review of my learning so far. It is still continuing but I feel I have reached a point for reflection, consolidation, and diffusion. I hope that those who wish to be more thoughtful and effective managers will gain helpful insights into what often happens at the top of organizations. It is the quality and application of thinking here that affects the daily life of all of us. Yet we rarely have sight of it and, even less frequently, debate it. I hope that this book will help the process of exposure and debate.

One small note on a matter of style before we start. I have used the term 'top managers' throughout to mean those people at the top of an organization who have the duty to give it direction and purpose. They may come from the main board, executive board, or subsidiary boards, amongst others. They will usually have the title of 'director' but many people have such a nominal, or statutory, title without ever giving direction in the 'general manager', non-specialist sense. What distinguishes direction-givers from the run of 'nominal' directors for me is that they have risen above their old specialist discipline, which took them up the organization, and have learned to cope across disciplinary boundaries with other specialisms about which they may know very little. They are the people who have learned how not to be fooled by experts from other disciplines, and how to enjoy and use the powers of uncertainty and ambiguity in their work.

'Senior managers' referred to in the text are those who have reached the top of their functional specialism but have not made the crucial step into becoming direction-giving general managers. They may well be called 'director', or have an even grander title, but they are not direction-givers in my terms. They are also some of the most dangerous managers I know. They are the people who, often unwittingly, maintain the status quo when change is needed because they do not have the perspective to see the consequences of following the present line. They ensure a slow death for their organization by not learning the direction-giving role. Unless organizations have top managers capable of spending a large proportion of their time looking and thinking ahead they are doomed to repeat the problems of the past. In a rapidly changing world past solutions have little to offer the future.

Part One

REFLECTIONS AND CONCEPTS

Section One
What is the Problem?

Non-Performing Directors

'If I had known just how unsupportive people would be, I'm not
sure I would have taken this job . . . it's the one area where it is
assumed that no training is needed, so no training is provided . . .
what makes it worse is that everyone assumes you know what's
going on. They all have political reasons for withholding information from you so you never really "know" anything. It's the
most lonely and frustrating of positions.' Chief executive, US food
processing corporation.

'The daft thing is that you work for high office throughout your
career. You become more and more specialist and more and more
valued. Then you are finally promoted to the board, get your title
and all the perks, only to find that it's a hollow joke. You are
suddenly expected to be omniscient. You are meant to know
everything about everything. The truth is that you know a lot
about very little because you have become so specialized. At this
level you need to feel that you will not be fooled by other
specialists – but that does not happen. Yet there seems to be no
way of saying "help!" so people at the top often feel uncomfortable, resentful, and cannot do what they are paid to do.' Managing director, UK engineering company.

These quotations are just two of many that I have collected over
the last decade. They indicate a structural flaw in the design and
development of our organizations. As these are the basis of modern society, the problem is worthy of some thought.

The most regular comment I get from directors of businesses of
all sizes is that they really do not know precisely what it is they
should be doing as a director rather than a specialist. They often
feel that they somehow should not be there, are rather frightened

25

of 'being found out', and are frustrated that at the very moment when their career appears to be at its peak, as far as the external world is concerned, a feeling of insecurity, stress, incompleteness, and being cheated is present. Such feelings do nothing for the confident and competent exercise of the key responsibility and duty of a director – to give direction to the organization.

In my work these feelings have been confided to me so many times that they do seem to be characteristic of directors across the world – in the United Kingdom, continental Europe, the United States, Hong Kong, Malaysia, and even China. Independent support for my observations comes from research work undertaken by BUPA, the private health care organization. They found that by far the most significant cause of stress in executives is not found in those areas of corporate folklore which form the received wisdom about stress – moving house, moving site, divorce, death of a loved one, etc. – but in overpromotion. It stood head and shoulders above the others and was particularly strong in top managers.

Once those feelings of insecurity, hollowness, and overpromotion are present, the emotional and behavioural consequences are insidious within an organization. All of us like to work from a position of 'comfort' in both a physical and emotional sense. When we move, or are moved, into an uncomfortable organizational position we try to learn how to cope and develop. If we cannot cope then we slip back into our old position of comfort, given half a chance. If the difficulties we encounter are major, then our behaviour will betray one or more of the signs of frustration: aggression; regression to an earlier form of behaviour; fixation on one answer or person to blame; or withdrawal from the issue. None of these are helpful to managerial problem-solving, yet they all have powerful driving forces behind them which if turned to their inverse can be highly creative. Aggression can become drive; regression can become a reframing of the problem statement; fixation can become a commitment to achieve a specific goal; and withdrawal can become a time to think and reflect. All of these are highly desirable qualities for people charged with directing a business. But I have yet to meet an organization which consciously sets out to develop such qualities in its directors.

To this extent the received wisdom of the workforce can be uncomfortably accurate. 'Top management don't have a clue what they are doing'; 'they do not understand the consequences of that decision taken in isolation'; 'don't they see the advantage we've handed our competitors?'; 'it seems that everyone can see the way the world is changing except them' – these are commonly heard laments in organizations all over the world. Such mutterings are symptomatic of two organizational issues – the failure to develop a thinking function at the top of the business; and, often forgotten because of the former, the desire of the members of that organization to see it survive and prosper.

These grumblings are perhaps proof of the Peter Principle – that people are promoted to their level of incompetence in organizations. The employees are aware of it. The directors are aware of it. But little happens. Why should that be so?

**Lack of Director Development:
Springing the Final Career Trap**

The questions I am regularly faced with in my consulting are how did we get ourselves into this level of frustration and literally thoughtlessness in the first place, and what can we do to get out of it?

Research work on the stages of maturity in a job[2] showed that, over time, people seemed to follow a natural sequence of events from their moment of entering a company, or job, through to their leaving it. My version of the sequence is:

Induction

Inclusion

Competence

Personal development

Plateau

Transition

My argument is that there is a 'natural' sequence of steps as one moves through a job. Each step needs to be addressed and worked upon until it is in reasonable balance before one can usefully go to the next stage. One cannot leapfrog stages either from a personal or an organizational viewpoint, no matter how much one, or the organization, insists it should be possible. Learning can only be achieved over time, even if we 'know' the answer and want to rush into action.

In most organizations the induction stage is fairly well handled, people are introduced to their new organization or job, the people with whom they will be working, and given some clues as to what is expected of them in terms of the technical side of their jobs. But many organizations do not handle the inclusion stage well. The underlying assumption behind this stage is that the work we do comprises two quite distinct aspects – the technical side for which expertise we are paid our salaries, and the social side. This latter provides the film of lubrication between us and the people with whom we work.

The inclusion stage is about building up rapport, trust, and credibility so that we can be accepted by and work with our fellows. Most organizations assume that inclusion will happen somehow, and put little energy or time into ensuring that it is effective. I believe that it is an important developmental stage which needs managing because, without it, it is impossible to become competent in an organization or job. The number of technically excellent specialists one finds in organizations who cannot handle the people side of managing, and are consequently rebuffed by their colleagues or other work groups, is legion. They are often characterized as 'too clever by half' and tend to spend a miserable time trying to thrust their obvious expertise on to unwilling audiences. They are some of the saddest people one finds in organizations.

Competence is only established once these technical and social relationships are built. Many people never become competent, in these terms, in an organization. A great deal of frustration is built up in them and this is made manifest through the odd and often bizarre behaviour with which organizations abound – a mixture of a desire to inflict harm on those who will not include them, and a strong wish not to be found out as incompetent.

It is not my wish here to go through all the career stages. When I talk with my director clients, it is usual only to get this far before all sorts of 'Aha!' and 'Now I see it!' noises are made. They get excited and draw for me analogies of the way their specialist, technical, career paths have developed through the total job stage cycle. They even replicate the process for their whole career – until they reach the very top. Then some fundamental flaws seem to show through. They are emotionally and conceptually blocked at the moment of the apparent achievement of their career goals. Shortly after, frustration sets in.

The most important aspect of the problem seems very simple. I know of no organization that has thought through two basic managerial concerns. First, they have not specified the performance expected of their directors. Second, they have not designed and operated an induction, inclusion, and developmental process for their top managers. There seems to be an implicit assumption in organizations that the very act of declaring someone a director or general manager somehow bestows on them the powers of omniscience. Suddenly they are expected to be able to understand and advise upon all matters regardless of specialist discipline. They are expected to be able to interpret political nuances in the external world in areas which have been usually banned to them before, and to understand the cultural subtleties of their company's international relationships even when their previous career has been insular in the extreme. If they cannot, it is usually suggested they keep quiet and let those who understand these things get on with them.

One managing director put it succinctly: 'The very specialists who previously bumped into mountains because they kept their eyes so far down are suddenly expected to leap them at one bound.' In the early days my biggest puzzle was why such people tolerated such an unsatisfactory state of affairs?

When questioned, the directors gave answers which tended to follow a distinct pattern. First, the new top managers would say how pleased they had been in being promoted and recognized for the quality of the work they had put in over what was usually many years. Then they would say that it was curious and disturbing for them to find that no one actually worked with them on their induction into the top team, nor on their inclusion. Moreover, the very notion of there being a 'top team' was often missing. It felt more like a collection of disparate specialist disciplines fighting out a bid for power at the top of the organization, rather than any type of integrated thinking and directing mechanism. After a period of discomfort the new directors would usually conclude there was little chance of being able to become competent in the organization because no one seemed to know what was appropriate performance. So each in his or her own way sought a position of comfort to the detriment of the organization as a whole.

The key issues seemed to be that most directors did not see themselves as competent in their directing role; found it difficult to understand what constituted effective performance in the new role; could see little chance of getting help with developing such a role; felt resentment at being put in such an uncomfortable position; and adopted behaviour which hid such feelings and thoughts from colleagues, superiors and subordinates. All of this meant that they were in no frame of mind to learn how to cope with monitoring the external environment, integrating the specialist functions of a business, nor to develop their subordinates to do their old job well.

When discussing this with company chairmen and chief executives they often express their frustration at what they see as 'wet' or 'wimpish' behaviour by newly appointed directors and general managers. They reflect that they had to face such issues and had to develop themselves in the best ways that they could. This is true. Yet they often acknowledge that it was a hit-and-miss affair, heavily dependent on luck, and that it would not have taken much thought or investment to have had a much more manageable and effective process with obvious personal and organizational benefits. But it does take thought and investment.

The Need to Clarify the Director's Role

The major comment of directors across the globe was: 'We do not really know what it is that we are meant to do.' In one sense this was a nonsense as the duties of a director of a business are spelled out in Company Law in all countries.[3] These statutory duties are geared essentially to ensure that no criminal actions are taken on behalf of the company, and to ensure that shareholders' and employees' civil rights are maintained.

To this extent they are laudable. But such laws do not attempt to look at the issue of personal performance in the role of directing. It is difficult, and unwise, for the law to involve itself in such areas. However, it is of great importance for the owners and employees to have a model and measures by which they can compare and contrast the performance of the people selected to run the business.

It is here that one begins to sense the vacuum. When asking what it is that defines the competent exercise of the director's role, all sorts of answers are given. These would include that the product or service is properly defined; that sufficient return on investment is generated to please the shareholders; that the business is run efficiently so that costs are always kept low; that pay and conditions are the highest possible to ensure the retention of a qualified workforce; that markets are carefully addressed so that the company has a competitive edge over others; that there is time to think built into the organizational processes; and many others.

These are all necessary but are they enough? It seemed to me that they were all subsets of a more fundamental need and structure. What this is has taken me a long time to track down. But like all simple discoveries, it was staring me in the face – if only I had known what to look for.

Section Two
Why Does It Matter?

It is a received organizational truth of many Western businesses, and some Oriental ones, that people are promoted to their level of incompetence. The words used are usually stronger and form part of the organizational oral tradition. From the workforce come the stories of their noble efforts being foiled because they are 'lions led by donkeys'. From top management there is a common lament characterized by the cry: 'We invested all that time and money getting him to the top of his professional tree, then promoted him into a managerial job which he hated, and in which we hated him. What is the logic in that?' What else could they have done?

Before we go much further let me expand on the term 'role'. I use it to mean more than just a job. A job is what we start with, it is what is stated in the job description. Politics and human nature adapt, erode, and manipulate this over time so that we become much more comfortable with it. We add our personality to the original specification, adding an unspecified bit here and losing a specified bit there. Provided that this is accepted by those above us and those with whom we work, it becomes our 'role' in the organization.

There are three reasons why it is important to pay attention to the role and development of the people at the top of a business. Each is usually treated as 'obvious' when mentioned in conversation. Yet the behaviour of most organizations is to accept the logic and then do nothing about it. Behaviour is the acid test of 'reason' – I do, therefore I think – but the reasoning is equally important – I think, therefore I do. It is to encourage the latter behaviour that I am writing this book.

The Hierarchy of Necessary Roles for Effective Organizations

There is a minimum of three types of role needed to allow any organization to perform effectively, to both think and do:

— Integrating and direction-giving

— External monitoring

— Operational planning and actions

Each is necessary and must be linked through a system of organizational learning to form a conscious and responsive whole.

Most people spend their working lives at the Operational Planning and Actions level. To them it is the whole of 'work'. They do not see, or seek, involvement in the other two levels, although they will have firm opinions about the quality of the people who are responsible for these activities.

But it is dangerous for any organization to be lulled into thinking that the Operational level is the only one worth considering. It does take up the bulk of time of 95 per cent of the members of an organization, but what happens in the other 5 per cent is crucial to organizational survival. If this is not recognized then the business will die over time – and there are many dying organizations. The tragedy is that often their directors are unaware of the fact.

The External Monitoring level is often left to the sales force, sometimes wrongly under the title of 'marketing', or to the research and development functions. However, it is rarely seen as an adjunct of the policy planning, or strategic positioning, function of a business and, in truth, in many organizations the function does not exist. When it does, it is rarely part of a conscious organizational system of learning about, and adapting to, the dynamics of the wider environment.

The Integrating and Direction-giving level performs the 'brain' function of a business. It monitors what is happening in day-to-day operations, checks what is happening in the wider environment, and then takes decisions on how best to deploy the limited resources it controls to achieve its objectives in the given conditions.

It is the core of information processing and consciousness in the business. As such it is the key role of the directors.

It is this direction-giving level that seems to cause problems in organizations. It is also the one which disorientates those senior managers who are promoted into it from the top of their specialist function without preparation. They are exposed to a range of disciplines and other experts over whom they have apparent control but little knowledge or skill with which to ask apposite questions. Indeed there is a great deal of evidence that such people are regularly fooled by these experts as they have perfected the art of baffling directors through the use of an excluding technical language – 'techno-babble'.

Coming to terms with asking the right questions seems crucial to understanding the directing-giving role. As Reg Revans, the doyen of action learning,[4] put it so pithily: 'We have to have experts to find answers to the difficult questions, but what I am interested in is who is going to ask the right bloody questions?'

In my experience there seems to be a great deal of energy spent avoiding the integrating/direction-giving role across the organizational spectrum, and the problem is by no means an exclusively British one. The issue of top managers never becoming comfortable with their directing role occurs across the world. It was reinforced powerfully when I was talking with colleagues from the Centre For Creative Leadership, Greensboro, North Carolina.[5] We are all involved in work on the perceived effectiveness of chief executives. There seems to be a remarkably common pattern. When people were promoted to the chief executive role they usually entered a period of wanting to be seen to make substantial changes, triggered by their predetermined notions of what was needed to make the organization more effective. These changes were a sign of perceived effectiveness in the new chief executive both for those who had made the selection and for those on the receiving end. Their initial expectations were met.

After about six months the first consequences of the rapid, often bold, changes seemed to start coming home to roost. The information base on which the decisions were taken was shown as slim. The layer of social lubrication necessary to ensure effective change had rarely been considered in the early excitement, with the result that overheating of the human processes in the organization occurred. This mixture of inadequate analysis and apparent disregard for the existing organizational culture and learning is dangerous. It requires deft handling.

A series of deviations from the early plans seem then to occur which can take various forms – deadlines are missed on new products or services, budgets are found to be inadequate and are overspent, labour problems mount, the reading of the market is inadequate so forecasts are unreliable. This leads to incorrect manufacturing and selling levels, which leads to incorrect inventory levels, which disrupts the cash flow, which invalidates the financing, and so on. Such combinations and consequences begin to change the perceived effectiveness of the new chief executive into perceived ineffectiveness. This period is tough as his or her credibility is eroded rapidly and an 'I told you so' mentality pervades the organization.

The researches seem to show that it then takes about eighteen months for the chief executive to build an effective system which blends his or her wishes with the culture and aspirations of the people who comprise the organization. This process of consciously rebuilding credibility and being more aware of the realities of the organization takes time before a balanced achieving and nurturing culture can be created. But if the direction-giving and ideas are there, and the behaviour at the top fits the words spoken to encourage the workforce to follow the proffered leadership, then highly effective organizations can emerge.

The joke is that some research also shows that in the current turbulent circumstances the normal period within which a chief executive moves on from the organization is between twenty-four and thirty months. Hence, after the early honeymoon period, it is rare for a chief executive ever to be seen as highly effective. This must explain at least part of their frustration. When I talk about this pattern I usually get a 100 per cent response of 'that is how it was for me' from top managers. They often felt resentful that just at the point they were learning how to lead their organization they were moved on, or kicked out, so that the learning was lost and someone else was brought in to repeat the pattern, with slightly different mistakes, all over again.

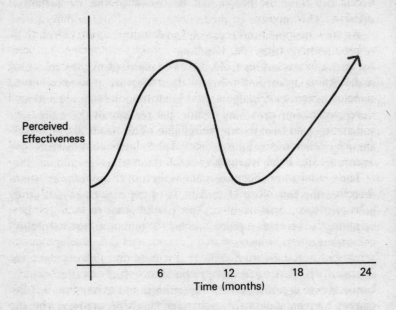

Perceived effectiveness of incoming chief executives

Directors as Blockages to Development

Given that defining hierarchical roles is necessary to create a learning organization, and positioning the directors so that they can achieve their direction-giving role, the second reason why it is important to define a clear role for directors is that without one they impinge on, and blur, other people's roles.

I have mentioned previously that because of the lack of induction and inclusion processes in organizations, when directors take up their new job they have a hard time becoming competent. After a time they seek their position of comfort. This is usually their old job, at the head of the specialist function through which they had progressed for most of their organizational life. They retreat into that job and feel good about it because they have something discernible to do. However, their return does not necessarily make the people in their old functional department or division feel so good.

As the functional head receives the promotion to director, a chain of promotions is triggered. This is part of the developmental process for an organization which, if handled creatively, can ensure a strong and learning-inclined workforce. The return of a non-performing director, albeit unofficially, to his or her old job blocks this natural developmental process. You cannot have two people doing the same job and hope to have it done well. Fights occur about who should do the job, relations are soured, career development is blocked and unconstructive behaviour becomes the norm.

The organizational consequence is that, over time, the return of directors to their old jobs means that people are paid for doing jobs one, two, or even three levels below that of their job description. This creates a resentful attitude amongst the members of the organization, which, in turn, encourages the development of micro-political infighting. All of this is to the detriment of the organization. Part of the integrating/direction-giving function of a business is to create a culture where this does not happen. But this cannot happen unless the right climate exists amongst the top management.

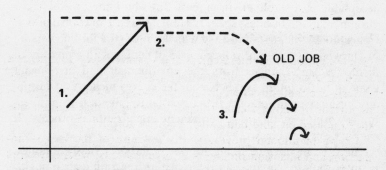

The knock-on effects of directors slipping back into their old jobs.

Key: 1 — New director is frustrated by inability to fully grasp new job
2 — Hiatus is resolved by unofficially moving back into old job
3 — Persons promoted to new jobs are, in turn, blocked by their inability to be responsible for them

The Danger of Creating 'Bourbon' Organizations

The third reason for clarifying the role of directors is to encourage a climate and system of learning in the organization. If an organization's directors are uncomfortable about using their integrating/direction-giving powers, and career development is slowed down or blocked, then it is hardly likely that the right mood exists in which to learn about change.

Yet the changes inside and outside a business determine those very 'energy niches' which ensure its survival through adaptation and competitiveness. If it is not possible for an organism to learn, then it will not survive. That is why having a brain is such an evolutionary competitive advantage. Without a brain capable of abstractions we would be reduced to sign/stimulus predetermined behaviour insufficient to cope with our environmental changes.

I am puzzled as to why so many organizations try to behave as though they did not need a brain function. Many seem to prefer to operate with their corporate eyes and ears closed, and with a quiverful of retribution for those who try to say, 'Wait a minute, let's look at what is going on out there'. The common response is: 'We cannot deal with any new information because we are so busy processing and using what we have already collected.' This is acceptable in a stable environment. But who knows a stable environment in the business sphere? Here it is a case of evolve or die. Conceptually we are not dealing with a simple straight-line version of Darwinian evolution, rather a case of coping with a mixture of disruptive step-changes from the environment and an elegant game of tit for tat in, and between, the energy niches that sustain any business environment. It is essential to have a true business brain working at this as a permanent organizational process. It cannot be left to chance.

There is an obvious liking for the Bourbon dynasty amongst many corporate leaders – a preference for reaction over thought. It was said of the Bourbons that 'they learned nothing, and they forgot nothing'. I have the feeling that this is the preferred position of many top managers. They appear to prefer binary thinking methods (something is either good or it must be bad) to more subtle processes. Yet in a changing world this is a patently absurd position to adopt. What can be done to ensure that such climates are not replicated, both in those existing organizations which still have some hope of learning and in the new organizations which will carry us into the twenty-first century?

Who Is Responsible for the Development of Directors?

There seems to be no mechanism in our society for monitoring or debating the exercise of the 'brain' function in an organization. In theory it should be easy because, above all, the shareholders and employees will want to know. In practice this seems not to be so. The shareholders, particularly the 'institutions', seem content to measure managerial effectiveness on such short-term issues as profit and dividend growth. These are essentially depersonalized yardsticks. They do not measure the quality of managerial thought and action nor the longer-term ability to successfully guide the business towards market share and continuing product development.

Matters were easier for the old-established 'dynastic' family firms because the people who rose to the top had been socialized from birth to the kind of thinking necessary to retain and nurture the family 'heritage'. With the growth of modern corporations, shareholders and their agents (the managers) have been separated and the socialization process has been lost. It is considerably easier for shareholders to sell out and try another company rather than try to improve the one in which they have invested.

The share analysts tend to reinforce this reaction for they have few, if any, frameworks with which to measure the managerial dimensions of a business. The main board is directly, or indirectly, party to this process and often finds it difficult to be self-critical, particularly if it is also part of the executive function of the business. Lord Caldecote's aphorism – 'The trouble with British companies is that they mark their own examination papers' – is apposite. This creates a dilemma for any organization that tries to deal with the issue of organizational ineffectiveness at the very heart of its being.

The only group of people who do have a good idea of the nature and quality of what really happens in a business are those with the smallest voice – the employees. They face the daily consequences of the thinking and behaviour of top managers, but there is usually no process for debating, or feeding back, constructive criticism of what happens. So they tend to bear with it regretfully, and show just as frustrated behaviour as those at the top. Psychologically, the 'them and us' mentality is very easy to create. My experience is that it is slower, but not difficult, to dispel once credible and consistent thought and behaviour is shown by top managers. But to achieve a process of debating and reception of constructive criticism in organizations needs careful design to make it workable.

It is not just the lack of appropriate assessment of the boards, or the analysts, which obscures the problem of directors' responsibility. There are psychological and anthropological issues which have a bearing on the way people think about what happens at the top of an organization. The process of directing a business tends to be shrouded in myths and clouded by the expectation that it involves areas of arcane knowledge which must take years of apprenticeship to acquire. As with all such beliefs, there is an element of truth in them. However, many organizations seem to use such notions to obscure the fact that no one at the top is clear about what they are doing. New directors are told, 'Don't ask too many questions now as it takes time to understand these things, my boy'. Pressure is applied to serve time, rather than rock the boat by asking discriminating questions about what one is meant to be doing, which tends to lead to action rather than thought as a therapy for relieving the uncertainty.

Such an approach from the existing top team resembles the story of the Emperor's new clothes. It is not relevant on the long haul to directoral competence. What is relevant is a more difficult problem.

In the second part of this book I will review elements of thinking, learning, and design which I believe make a contribution to the competent exercise of the direction-giving function. Surprisingly little research work has been completed in this area and so very little that is theoretically strong and practically robust is widely diffused. This is not surprising because most organizations are only too well aware of the problems they have with their top managers and do not want this exposed. On the other hand there is a growing awareness that help is needed in this area.

In this part of the book I shall concentrate on what I see as the fundamental structures and thinking processes necessary to achieve the learning organization. It is noticeable that a search for such help is not easy. I am unaware of a single business school which runs programmes in the area of direction-giving and integrating that are rated highly by its participants. Most do not run programmes. Business schools and consultancies are just as prone to 'Bourbon' tendencies as other organizations. They have similar problems with functional specialists as do the corporations and so tend to limit their offerings to senior management levels where specialist can still speak to specialist. Top management programmes seem to be run on the basis that 'if we can give them enough specialists to listen to, then something must stick'. At this level they tend towards the sheep-dip approach to training. The higher notions of integration and design are not appreciated because these are not areas traditionally marked out as 'management studies'.

The problem of developing directors, as presented to me by clients, seems insoluble within the bounds set by current organizational thinking. The problem needs reframing to allow a different and wider perspective. My search for ideas and processes that will help has been eclectic. It goes way beyond the borders of traditional management studies and enters such fields as ecology, anthropology, political science, learning theory and, most of all, design. When stated in such bald terms it can induce in 'straight' top managers both ridicule and panic. Taken slowly and with a strong theoretical backing, rooted in practice, I know that what I have stated can make a profound difference to all members of an organization through changing dramatically their roles, output, and effectiveness.

The crucial responsibility for ensuring the survival and growth of organizations usually falls neatly between the stools of ownership and management in most organizations. Typical responses from the parties involved are:

Reflections and Concepts

Shareholders

– either see themselves as too fragmented and out of touch to be able or willing to influence matters or, if institutional shareholders, say that their power is only to comment on overall rather than individual performance and express this through buying or selling the shares.

Non-Executive Directors

– usually see themselves as too isolated and powerless to make constructively critical comments on the individual and group performance of boards. Only in the more far-sighted companies is this seen as a key role for them.

Chairman

– often feels that this is beyond his/her remit as it should logically fall into the responsibilities of the chief executive. The chairman will sometimes accept a personal counselling or mentoring role.

Chief Executives

– often accept that they should do more to develop their colleagues but cannot see how they can find the time or resources, particularly when pressed for short-term profits. Many neither understand nor value the process sufficiently to invest in it. Moreover, by having isolated 'directionless' directors failing to perform their proper organizational role a chief executive can maintain one-person rule. In this case 'top team development' is very unwelcome.

Executive Directors

– often the 'directionless' ones. With all the other persons involved having little information about, or commitment to, director development, the truth seems to be that the only people with an interest are the directors themselves. If they wish to learn their role they will need to combine to form a coalition of learning to develop both the personal and organizational development processes. If not, then the organization will have its executive directors developed from outside by people with a vested interest in seeing that some development is carried out – *the headhunters*!

Whilst reliable statistics are hard to come by to assess turnover rates for directors, it is reasonable to assume that on average they will, like many other managers, change their jobs every three years. Many of these will be internal changes but my talks with top managers, particularly since 1980, would suggest that some 50 per cent of UK top managers have changed jobs through headhunters in the past five years. In companies where this has not happened there are no grounds for complacency. If they are failing to develop competent directors, then their staff are as liable to be the prey of executive search as anyone.

Section Three
What Can Be Done?

To achieve more effective and efficient organizations through more competent and confident directors three issues must be addressed:

1. The roles of the directors need to be clarified and publicized within their organization.
2. There must be an organizational structural design which incorporates the learning process at its core.
3. There must be developmental processes available so that each member of the organization, from the top to the bottom, can learn to accept the rights and duties of his or her position.

These issues are relatively easy to identify, but they are less easy to achieve. Care needs to be spent ensuring that the organizational climate is conducive to achieving these aspirations, i.e. that the conditions under which people will be keen to learn are present. These conditions can be described as follows:

1. That there is a public recognition that the right conditions are needed for the good of the whole, as well as individual needs.
2. That encouragement will be given to those who set out to achieve the new roles, and that it is acknowledged that this will mean some degree of risk and failure whilst the learning is happening, so 'cover' will be given to those ready to learn.
3. That monitoring and appraisal will be on an agreed and universally applied system in which the perceived behaviour of people is given priority.

The skills of managing organizational climate, and the constructive conditions for learning, are dealt with later in this book. Here I want to deal with the issue of what we can do about directors' roles, and helpful organizational models for reinforcing these.

'We was robbed!'

This is a cry often uttered, only half-jokingly, when directors describe reaching the pinnacle of their career. They talk of having spent a lifetime moving up their specialist tree and describe this, using their hands, as a progression towards the tip of a pyramid – 'knowing more and more about less and less'. The feeling of being robbed is triggered because built into the organizational values was the idea that this was how people reached the top, and that they would be rewarded for so doing. The sting is in that tail. Having got to the top they describe it by pushing their hands wide apart – 'To do our work properly we are suddenly expected to enter a new game, after twenty or thirty years of the old one, and a game about which we know little and are helped less'.

What interests me for this part of the book are the dimensions of that new game. There is no doubt that in many organizations there exists at all levels the expectation that the directors will be the direction-giving part of the business, from which all others will take their lead. That this rarely happens is irrelevant to this part of the argument. The crux is that this is the usual expectation. Irrelevant too is the fact that most organizations promote to this key activity people who are unlikely to be able to perform it, unless given a large amount of help. This process of mis-selection leads to low morale in the workforce as the directors behave according to, and reinforce, the cynical organizational stereotypes of them.

The directors are aware of their lacunae but are unwilling to voice their need to learn for fear of being seen as wrongly promoted. The people not being given direction see that nothing is being learned at the core of the organization and adopt blocking or apathetic behaviour. How can this unsatisfactory state of affairs be overcome?

Turning Specialists into Generalists

The fundamental problem is in reframing the role of the director from being a specialist to becoming comfortable with being a generalist. In all organizations the mix of specialism and generalism will be different. The necessary psychological condition is for directors to be willing to start letting go of some of their deeply learned specialist thoughts and behaviour, to allow time and space for the learning of new attitudes, knowledge and skills.

In disciplinary terms this can be uncomfortable as the new areas tend to be integrative rather than clearly differentiated. Many specialists are trained to exclude areas of knowledge, skills and attitudes throughout their training and professional life, so the idea of accepting and valuing areas previously excluded is a difficult one and liable to be rejected unless handled carefully.

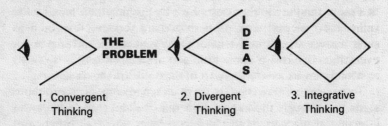

1. Convergent   2. Divergent   3. Integrative
   Thinking   Thinking   Thinking

Convergent, divergent, and integrative thinking

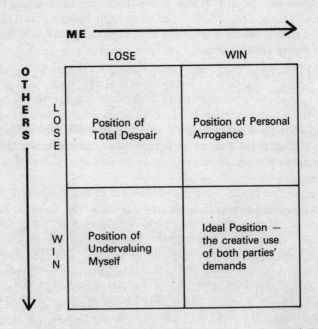

Changing 'either/or' to 'both . . . and'

The essence of the generalist approach seems to be found in consciously stopping the inbuilt professional tendency to exclude, compartmentalize, and label – to fight what Tom Wolfe has called 'campus thinking'.[6] This process is deeply rooted within most managers and is characterized in many ways. In the daily language of organizations it is found in the 'it's not my responsibility' or the 'it's more than my job's worth to do that' type of attitude. In the rather more elegant terms of management theorists it is found in such notions as Alistair Mant's 'binary manager'[7] who will see everything in terms of 'either/or'. Once such thinking is regularly reinforced by successful behaviour, it is difficult to move.

To move from 'either/or' to 'both . . . and' is tricky. It requires some new thought processes which will be dealt with more deeply later in the second part of this book. More importantly for now, the change in thinking processes requires different values becoming commonly used by directors. Amongst these are:

1. Valuing differences and becoming comfortable with enjoying using them.

2. Learning to value the asking of discriminating questions of experts, rather than valuing depth of knowledge for its own sake.

3. Learning to value the skills and attitudes needed to set managerial questions in their broader economic, social, and political contexts.

The essence of the move is to break out of the old 'binary' style of thinking and to rise above it to an 'issue and context' based approach. Alistair Mant in his *The Rise and Fall of the British Manager* points out that many managers can get themselves trapped into inappropriate patterns of thinking and behaviour by believing on the one hand that it is sufficient to just 'be' a manager rather than demonstrate this by 'doing' the managerial job and, on the other hand, by feeling that only binary thinking is 'right'.

Binary thinking is the process whereby all matters are reduced to polar opposites – things are either good or they are bad; right or wrong; black or white. The belief is that this is good because it

47

clarifies matters and leads to fast and easy resolution of problems. It does no such thing. It works on a similar principle to the notion that if you have only a hammer, then all problems tend to look like nails. This is unhelpful when you are involved in delicate political discussions which demand that you spend more time influencing others, like customers or colleagues, rather than telling them what to do.

Binary thinking is a crude and dangerous tool which can reduce all managerial thinking to the level of interpersonal feuding – to win/lose battles. At the strategic and policy-making levels it is particularly unhelpful. There is little subtlety in it, and it precludes the opportunity to use the uncertainties and ambiguities in any situation to creative advantage. It tends to *reducto ad absurdum*. Yet many organizations are managed in this way. This is the primrose path to the Bourbon bonfire.

What seems to work more effectively is the 'both . . . and' style of thinking. Mike Pedler and Tom Boydell deal with this in their book *Managing Yourself*[8] in the Fontana series so here I will mention the essence of being more demanding of the situation (I want this *and* that) and more design-orientated in one's thinking processes (now how can I achieve both?). This leads to richer and more subtle solutions – the director is paid above all to ensure the quality of organizational problem-solving – and it encourages the use of the creative and synthesizing process of synergy ($2+2=5$) rather than the demeaning process of reductionism ($3-2=1$).

Coping With Tolerance and Uncertainty

'Both . . . and' thinking means that a director needs to cope with a lot more uncertainty and ambiguity in his or her managing and design processes. Later I will argue that this is a key to successful direction-giving. Here I will say only that it is important to learn ways of becoming comfortable with the idea of the world as a turbulent and uncertain place in which major disruptive forces are constantly reshaping the energy niche within which the business exists. Whilst it is possible to build 'fortress' type organizations to resist the dynamics of environmental change, the energy and investment needed to do so are enormous. My question for directors is: 'Is it worthwhile to do so when the alternative is to set up a system of organizational learning to which all members can contribute, and which will keep you moving with the flows rather than investing in resisting them?'

Looking Upwards and Outwards

This returns us to a central issue for directors of specialism and generalism. If one is to raise one's eyes from the close focus of one's specialism, then two other distinct perspectives are seen. In the middle ground is the need to integrate other specialisms to allow synergy to operate at the core of the business. I will return to this aspect later in this section.

On the horizon are the national and international affairs of the world which impinge on our daily work, but which we tend to ignore out of lack of awareness or in the belief that there is little we can do about them. It is here that processes are being developed by companies to help directors realize that these potential disruptions in the wider environment are important to monitor, analyse, and take action on if one is to give direction. It is in this external environment that I find effective directors spend time regularly monitoring and debating changes, and adjusting their plans to allow flexibility to manoeuvre.

Most businesses are inherently inward-looking and so the nature of most organizational fights are essentially interpersonal – the issue reduced to personalities, just like the tabloid press. Any issue is quickly reduced, via the binary thinking process, to personalized battles between individuals or departments during which logic, rationality, and the issue itself are lost. Mant describes this blinkered world with the symbol:

Such organizations can resemble Matthew Arnold's 'Dover Beach', having

> . . . really neither joy, nor love, nor light,
> Nor certitude, nor peace, nor help for pain;
> And we are here as on a darkling plain
> Swept with confused alarms of struggle and flight,
> Where ignorant armies clash by night.

It is necessary to transcend such binary thinking if one is to get a proper perspective of an issue. It is significant, for example, that the Shell Oil Company searches for 'helicopter vision' in its most able managers. It is this ability to rise above the immediate and personalized issues, to see the wider perspective of what is important for better quality organizational solutions, that characterizes effective directors.

To develop this ability it is essential to learn to identify the 'issue' in any problem or dispute, to depersonalize it, and to use it as the vehicle through which to have the 'fight'. In this manner more energy is put into important problems, and less into personalized feuding, so better quality problem-solving is likely to emerge. Mant invented a new symbol to characterize this process:

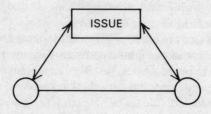

Coping With the Outside World

'It's all very well your saying that we should spend more time reading the newspapers each day to check what's going on in the world and how it might affect us but I never have time to do it . . . and anyway I really wouldn't know where to start!' Operations director, heavy engineering company.

This response is understandable. As soon as we lift our eyes from the specialist fields the world looks very large, intimidating, and incomprehensible because we do not have easy frames of reference with which to interpret what is happening. But the response is not acceptable if we are to create an effective organization.

I am working currently with a large financial services group. Out of their 30,000 staff they have identified some 200 potential top managers whom they wish to develop as the next generation of direction-givers for their businesses. We have resisted the immediate urge simply to expose them to the other specialist disciplines because this is seen as taking the traditional training, a 'more of the same' route. We want to change fundamentally people's perspectives so that they are more comfortable dealing with change and uncertainties, and can give effective direction.

To this end we have focused on Change as the key issue with which to start a re-education process. Under this heading three broad areas, not specialist disciplines, have been identified as providing the determinants of the world in which the group will have to exist in future:

Social change

Technological change

Economic change

and we have asked the participants to look at each with three distinct perspectives:

International

National

Industry sector

The results have been exciting and energizing for the potential directors. In a residential period on the programme they have immersed themselves in international, national, and industrial politics, faced social issues of great complexity, and reframed the ways in which they see their business contributing to the economic good. They have met and managed contributors from the highest to the lowest in the land, and found it constructive and enjoyable to the point that one finance director complained jokingly: 'You have ruined my train journey to work each morning. Previously I used to skim the paper, then doze or watch my fellow passengers. Now I actually read the thing and, what's worse, I am capable of linking just about any news item to my work. It really is too much!'

What gives me gentle amusement is that the reframing which the group and I have embarked upon was so fundamental that in many ways it is not 'management' at all. We went way beyond that particular piece of 'campus thinking' before we could ever return and consider the specialist disciplines necessary for future management. Had we listed initially the areas in which we wished to operate – international affairs, political science, anthropology, sociology, ecology, design – the chances are that the group powerbrokers, or the participants, would not have encouraged us to proceed. By adopting a pragmatic approach based on changes and perspectives we were actively encouraged to proceed, with cheering results.

This type of developmental process has been tried in a few other industries and was developed originally by Geoff Gaines at the General Electric Company. One of its great assets is that the participants have to integrate their thinking and learning sufficiently in a short time to present their findings, views, ideas, and proposals to main board directors who are encouraged, and prove keen, to debate the future direction and information base of the group.

This is a very powerful climate in which to develop the next generation of direction-givers for an organization.

It is significant that the disciplines listed above are rarely found in business schools or management consultancies. In both, 'campus thinking' seems to block their ability to develop directors. More importantly, the disciplines mentioned tend not towards reductionism and exclusion, but to their opposite. They are synthetic and integrative in nature, management as a design activity rather than management as the lowest common denominator. They thrive when operating with other disciplines on issues and problems. In this way they are very different from what has gone before in the field of 'management'.

A director, once given the opportunity, tends to appreciate the opportunities offered by the slings and arrows of outrageous fortune which comprise the external environment and which constantly disrupt his or her carefully made plans. Learning to cope with such movements proves quite difficult initially for many Westerners. It is paradoxical that, with a belief system that is essentially based on free will rather than determinisim, they complain of feeling 'helpless' and 'unable to control events' when faced with major external disruptions. Perhaps the more fatalistic Orientals have a useful model in their Yin/Yang symbol. They see two primary and opposed forces (good and bad, right and wrong) each applying constant dynamic pressure on the other. But each is equal and opposite so that the whole never totally unbalances. Should it ever do so, at the heart of each is the quintessence of the other:

The Yin/Yang symbol

This can be a useful model with which to begin to think about direction-giving. It allows that there are major forces in the environment which are pushing on each other, and over which one has little if any direct control. However, there is an idea of balance in the total system which helps determine the boundaries and there is the reassuring irony that if one power overcomes the other it would only find the essence of itself. This 'fatalistic' model is, I find, an attractive halfway house for directors who want to get out of the vicious circle of helplessness but cannot cope with the idea of designing their future. It helps with looking upwards and outwards, but in itself it is not enough.

Design Your World

The directors I rate as effective set out to design their world in the way they want it. They act on George Bernard Shaw's maxim, 'Get what you like or you get to like what you get'. There will be all sorts of disruptions and changes along the way, but they position themselves to predict the worst so that they can avoid that and they cope with what they cannot predict. The one thing they do not feel is helpless in the face of events. They always feel there is some room for manoeuvre and opportunity. They are aware of the Yin/Yang forces at work but do not accept them as absolute. They look for the contexts in which changes are occurring and secure the 'energy niche' for their organization which allows it to survive and grow.

Such 'designer directors' are not those with Gucci shoes, Lacoste shirts, Dunhill lighters, Lamy pens, or Rolex watches but are those who see their role as designing a future in which their organization can develop. It is for the encouragement of such people that I will outline a few of the existing developmental processes which seem effective.

Learning and Ecology

The study of ecology – living organisms in relation to each other and their environment – suggests to me some helpful models for directors. Three seem apt for relating an organism to its environment.

First, the formula popularized by Reg Revans, that for an organization to survive, its rate of learning must be equal to, or greater than, the rate of change in its external environment, is fundamental. This is expressed as:

$$L \geqslant C$$

And for me the key role of the direction-giver is to ensure that this is so. If the organization's rate of learning in relation to the rate of environmental change is not being monitored and learning is not being achieved sufficiently rapidly, then the organization will suffer brain death and eventually die. Said in this way the idea has been received enthusiastically by directors as it seems to 'legitimize' going beyond their specialisms, and encourages them to transcend the micro-politics of their organization. Yet when I point out that this puts learning at the heart of their organizational role, this can create some apprehension – at least until I point out that learning here does not on any account equal training.

Second, there is the ecological notion of 'sufficient difference', or Ashby's Law of Requisite Variety,[9] which I interpret to mean that for an organism to exist there must be sufficient difference within it to allow it to cope with change. Too much similarity reduces the ability to adapt and learn. This idea is often received glumly by 'top teams', particularly those comprised mainly of engineers, financiers, bankers, and salesmen.

Third, the previously mentioned idea of the 'energy niche' is important in understanding the positioning of a business in relation to its external environment. The idea that an organization is supported from above, below, and on each side by other organizations who make up a system is often perceived only dimly by directors. The notion that relatively small changes in that system can affect the total can seem quite threatening to them, particularly if they are binary, and fatalistic, thinkers rather than issue-based, contextual, opportunistic, designer-directors. I will return to this idea later in this section when I look at 'Developing Integrative Models of Organizations'.

Learning as the Key to Future Business

Times have changed dramatically since the anti-learning statement by the chief executive of the telecommunications company mentioned in the Introduction. Then the idea that learning was a serious area of managerial study and development would have been laughed out of court. Now the $L \geqslant C$ model of action learning is seen increasingly around the world as a symbol of effective management. It is found in boardrooms and on the shop floor, in technical disciplines and in integrative ones. Since 1974 it has had a powerful and almost unpublicized effect on British management thinking.

Twelve years ago the leaders of the scorn-pourers were lawyers and financial managers. They could see little benefit for an organization, and even less to their professional practice, in taking 'learning' seriously. They rarely used the change (social, technological, economic) and context (international, national, industry sector) matrix to monitor and debate potential disruptions. Things have moved a long way since then.

The world recession since 1979, together with government policies, have forced the $L \geqslant C$ model into the consciousness of thinking top managers. Some could not cope and their businesses went under, with devastating effects on employment. Those who survived may not describe what happened in the terms I use; they tend towards such descriptions as 'the shake-out', 'drastic slimming down', 'retrenching', and 'consolidating'. Whatever the term used, the process was of a drastic reconsideration of objectives, strategies, operations, and resources. It is estimated, although the information is difficult to ascertain, that since 1980 more than half of UK directors have left their businesses through retirements or sackings. Remembering that of those remaining, over half have changed jobs in the last four years to 1985, one can see that the rate of change at the top of UK companies has been dramatic. My question is, 'What has been learned?'

Rather to my surprise it is the lawyers and financiers who are now making the running on behalf of learning, though they do not phrase it that way. The need for new designs in products, services, and processes has forced reconsideration of what it is that a company owns in terms of ideas, artefacts, and skills – its 'intellectual property'. This reconsideration has been compounded by foreign customers becoming more discriminating in the terms of selection of their suppliers. Whilst old-style imperialism disappeared some decades ago, modern technological imperialism as practised by Europe, the USA, and Japan is still around and can lead to major trading problems which centre on the cultural aspects of learning transfer.

Many Western companies are lax in their codification of their know-how and know-why, despite often massive investment in them. When the companies provide the complete artefact or service, this internal laxness is no particular problem to them. Now many of the newly industrialized countries (especially in South-East Asia), and some Third World countries, can provide manufacturing capacity backed with cheap labour rates which allow goods to be made almost anywhere in the world. The key to profitable trade is to get the know-how to do this. This puts the emphasis for business survival and development firmly on design and learning rather than manufacture. Hence the current demand from such countries for 'technology transfer' agreements. These rarely lead to a satisfactory outcome as cross-cultural issues arise which leave both parties frustrated. The providers become angry that ever-increasing demands are made to get at the very heart of their intellectual property rights – the research and development efforts on which their survival depends – whilst the recipients feel that what is transferred is only the technical side of the transfer equation, that the providers are holding back on the real know-why for which the recipients thought they had paid.

What does this mean for organizational learning? It is now the lawyers and financiers who realize that Western organizations are awash with learning about products and processes. However, the small amount of attention paid to codifying consciously and rigorously and to protecting that learning is causing concern, even in high-tech industries. Hence the rise of 'intellectual property' as a modern business issue. The ideas, processes, artefacts, know-how and know-why which can be protected by patent, copyright, trademark or other intellectual property rights are now of crucial importance to businesses. Unless they can be protected, anyone with the manufacturing capacity could go ahead and produce them, as the Guccis, Lacostes, IBMs, Dunlops, and Sonys know only too well. So 'IPRs' have become of such importance that learning, specifically its codification and diffusion, has become a central concern of top management. Whilst this fascinates some directors, it worries many, particularly as the diffusion process enters the strange fields of anthropology and sociology. They rarely see this as what they had entered business to do. Many argue that they joined specifically to avoid such things.

Coping With Change

Whilst learning is beginning to be seen as essential to business survival and growth, and therefore acceptable, the other side of the L $\geqslant$ C model, change, tends to be viewed as a necessary evil by many directors. It is rarely seen as an opportunity for rethinking and reframing what happens in an organization. Interestingly, the character for 'change' or problem in Chinese is the same as for 'opportunity' or, to be more precise, 'dangerous opportunity'. Most directors I meet tend to fixate on the danger rather than the opportunity and so adopt defensive poses. Even those who have broken out of this fixation find that trying to be more constructive is not sufficient. Recently a group sales manager, whose departments were undergoing major surgery, said, 'I'm so surrounded by "opportunities" that I'm up to my neck in them and slowly going under!'

Coping with change seems to need a rather different set of attitudes and thinking processes than those found in many people selected to be directors.[10] Here I am concerned with two basic notions of change which allow 'dangerous opportunities' to be grasped. Both can then be built into a robust organizational model of directing.

First- and Second-Order Change

The excellent work of the 'brief therapists' in the US has shown two key aspects to understanding and coping with change. First, that to start even a large change process often takes some minute changes to behaviour rather than massive analytical thought. Once these small adaptations become comfortable one can build large edifices, slowly, using behavioural building blocks. The therapists' work on agoraphobics could be an analogy for inward-looking directors. You cannot ask them to go out into the wide world on first meeting; the result would be disastrous. However, after a brief session building confidence, you can walk with them to the front door, and even open it and look out. Once this has been done a few times it is possible to put a foot over the doorstep, and so on. What brief therapy is not is analysis-paralysis. It does not ask the immobilizing question 'Why?' but concentrates on the more constructive 'What can be done?' and 'How can it be done?'. Such an approach seems to work well for the directors with whom I have dealt. Analysis has its place, but these directors do not see the wisdom of lying on an organizational couch for seven years whilst 'Why?' is asked of them. They tend to find pragmatism more to their taste than Freud or Jung.

It is interesting to compare this step by step, iterative approach with the bold, rapid change model described earlier. This can reassure the powerbrokers looking for effective change in the short term but seems to have little firm basis on the social/emotional side, with the result that the organization strikes back. The brief therapy approach is less dramatic in the short term but I would argue highly effective in the medium and long term.

The second aspect of change, described by Watzlawick, Weakland, and Fisch in their seminal book *Change*,[11] is that most people so restrict their frame of reference, or context, for the problem they are facing that little true change can occur. They get into such a routine with their work that they view virtually all problems in a similar way – back to all problems looking like nails when all you have is a hammer. Consequently, when asked to change matters, they tend to operate in a confined 'single loop' of learning on which they can only do 'more of' or 'less of' the same thing because of the given context. This is 'first-order change', and is essentially binary and, therefore, unhelpful for managerial problem-solving. Little learning can occur as little changes in the wider system – of which the present problem is an unlubricated part.

Matters only really change if one looks upwards and outwards away from the immediate symptoms and sets the problem in a wider context. We know through such processes as neuro-linguistic programming that the very act of looking up can help seriously ill people. It seems part of the natural healing process. When therapeutic action is combined with looking outwards, it allows us to get a better perspective of where we, and our problem, lie in relation to the wider world. We can get into our helicopter and hover above the problem, often marvelling at how small it and the people crying 'more of' or 'less of' really look. This process of setting the wider context and perspective is called 'reframing' and forms the crux of the idea of 'second-order change'. It allows us out of the problem as initially defined, raises the issues, depersonalizes the fights and allows movement through reframing the problem statement. This in turn allows a better allocation of energies to appropriate blockages or levers, so making significant movement possible. It is above all a way of thinking about problems in a way that transcends the routine thought processes of an organization.

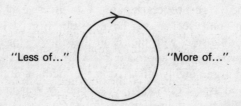

"Less of..."   "More of..."

First-order change

Second-order change

I wanted some way of describing first- and second-order change through a figure-of-eight shape, a double loop of learning, which would allow for continuous organizational learning processes. But I was aware of the political realities of organizations and the fact that it is rare to get all the members pointing in the same direction for any length of time.

Action learning sees change as an essentially political process in which it is necessary to design a coalition, however temporary, of the powers in an organization which have a vested interest in getting change to occur.

These 'temporary coalitions of power' comprise three elements which distil into three questions:

Who knows? — who has information about the problem? Not opinions, views, half-truths, official policies, but hard facts which will determine the dimensions of the problem.

Who cares? — who has the emotional investment in getting change made? Again, this is not who talks about the problem but who is involved in and committed to the outcome. These are often the people directly involved in current unsatisfactory work practices.

Who can? — who has the power to reorder resources so that changes can occur? Again, this is not a speculative matter, but one which confronts the issue of who, when faced with facts, commitment, and energy has the power to say 'Yes'.

It is my intention to go into more detail on this issue when dealing with developing organizational cultures in Part 2. For the moment I hope that it will prove sufficient to view change as an attitudinal and knowledge-reframing process which needs to be combined with the political process of coalition design for it to be effective. It is the director's role to ensure that the climate exists for this to happen.

Learning as the Key to Coping With Change

This brings us back to learning as a key process of survival and development in a business. The change processes described above are the political learning processes of an organization. This can cause some conceptual problems for directors who were educated via the 'hard', or technical specialist, route. They can become unnerved when words like 'political', 'ecological' and 'anthropological' are used. So I rarely use them, at least during the early stages of a project. Instead I tend to use the directors' admission of frustration at not being comfortable with their direction-giving role because of their tight, convergent, specialized thinking to raise the issue of what it is that blocks their ability to learn. Specifically, what blocks their coping with change?

Revans has highlighted the difference between 'clever managers' (technical specialists, or the experts) and 'wise managers' (those who ask good questions of their experts). He points out that much time and energy is spent in organizations erecting (in my terms) schools of 'campus thinkers' in which people get their satisfaction by being seen to be clever usually through putting down other (non-specialist) managers. Ultimately this process personalizes power struggles and leads first to a divide-and-rule climate and, later, a divide-and-die climate – where the lack of ability to ask integrating questions of the experts about issues which transcend the organization's micro-politics kills the ability to learn.

Revans argues that most specialist learning is of the highly codified ('programmed' or 'P') learning because the education system is designed to provide only that. What is needed for directors is the ability to ask discriminating questions – ('Q' learning) – of those experts so that specialist inputs can be maximized whilst the perspective is kept above all specialisms. Or, to put it in a more simple manner, the directors must learn to ask good quality questions so as not to be fooled by their experts. Revans plays upon the notion of 'looking after one's Ps and Qs' and describes the formula for organizational learning as $L = P + Q$.

Most directors seem to find this idea quite acceptable if a little disconcerting as they too come from specialist backgrounds. However, Revans is ready for them and describes in *The ABC of Action Learning*[12] the four major blockages to managerial learning – what he calls 'The Four Corrigible Handicaps':

1. The idealization of past experience

2. The charismatic influence of (other) successful managers

3. The impulsion to instant activity

4. The belittlement of subordinates

One can picture the type of director: one who believes that how things have been done before is more important than thinking about how they will be done in future; resistant to anything 'not invented here'; highly reliant on 'how we did it under old so-and-so'; focused more on instant and unthinking reaction rather than thoughtful and reflective proactivity; and failing to use and inspire subordinates in a manner which encourages them to their best efforts. I have come across many such directors in my consulting life.

Revans believes that each blockage must be tackled within the individual and the organization before effective learning can occur. I will argue later that the development of a 'learning culture' is a key role of the directors. The processes for moving people from the state described above to being comfortable with the learning culture encouragement role are all well tried. It is a slowish process, but consistent. Many organizations, however, seem to find it hard to take the first tiny behavioural step to break their anti-learning vicious circle and move it towards becoming a virtuous circle of learning. It takes time to value learning as an organizational necessity. I still find it ironic that it may now be thrust upon us through the lawyers and financiers who a decade ago seemed so resistant to the idea.

Developing Integrative Models of Organizations

It was noticeable during the 1960s and 1970s that the assumption was common amongst business people and management academics that a rigorous use of logic, rationality, and quantification was sufficient to solve any managerial problem. During this period there was a counter-culture which argued that the behaviour and aspirations of the people who comprised an organization were crucial to its performance. Concentrating on the people side, they argued, would give the conditions in which people would work well and feel part of their organization. These approaches were highly polarized and led to some bitter exchanges both in the business schools and in companies. The rational techno-economic approach usually won out because in the end the final score, the profits or surplus, was given in numbers so it was believed that everything must be reduced to these.

However, the 'scientific management' and quantitative schools of thought ran into severe problems during the middle 1970s. Whilst the final assessment of performance had to be given in numbers, which was necessary under the laws, they were not enough to get a grip on what was happening in an organization. Indeed the scientific value of something needing to be both 'necessary and sufficient' before it had universal applicability seemed forgotten by both sides in the binary thinking of the last twenty years.

The 'management scientists' were repeatedly attacked by 'true' scientists for being pseudo-scientists, because they had so few fundamental laws with which to map and describe the areas of their science. The arrival of cheap computing allowed a decade to pass whilst the quantifiers had their head and tried to reduce the process of organizing and managing to a series of logical formulae. Although some interesting progress was made, the general opinion inside businesses seems to be that it did not work. The attacks on the quantifiers became stronger and were reflected in other fields. Development economists found that their macro-economic models were not sufficient to cope with the desire to grow and diversify the economies of the less-developed countries. Econometricians found that their models of how an economy should behave did not fit reality. On the contrary, they were regularly confounded by it. Some writers in the *Harvard Business Review*[13] even attacked the analysis-paralysis and case-study base of Harvard itself – the very model of what a business school had been thought to be.

In the prestigious world of corporate planning the sounds of '*mea culpa*' and 'we've been duped' echoed around boardroom walls and the epitome of corporate strategy, Igor Ansoff, wrote: 'Over the past twenty years, it has become increasingly clear through lessons of success and failures, as well as through continuing research, that the Cartesian conception of the strategic problem suffers from two major deficiencies. First, in the language of management science, it is an 'improper optimization' – the excluded variables have major impact on the preferred solution. Second, strategic planning solves only part of the total problem concerned with maintenance of a viable and effective relationship between the organization and the environment.'[14]

Or, to put it another way, the areas which many had considered to be 'management studies' could not cope with the problems which organizations faced in the 1970s and 1980s. What else was needed to expand and integrate the domain of 'management' so that the excluded variables were included?

The easy way out was to add yet more functional disciplines to the top of a business. Whilst accountants continued to rule the roost it was noticeable that operations, marketing, sales, and personnel had a lot more attention paid to them in the 1970s. A definite shift occurred which allowed the more 'people-orientated' disciplines to play a growing part in designing and implementing the strategies for organizations. Cold logic had proved insufficient whilst emotions, the quality of strategic thinking, and the quality of working life began to become issues which boards tried to address.

Many directors saw this purely in terms of the micro-politics of their organization – whose functional star was waxing, and whose waning? Were Finance still in power? Or had Marketing ousted them? Would Planning ever get out of their back room and seize the commanding heights? Would Personnel be left on the back burner for ever? Were Data Processing on their way down after their failed attempts to deliver the world?

My view was rather different. I felt that major changes were under way which assumed a more integrated view of work in society, which included the generation and distribution of wealth in ways which the previous generation of directors had not considered. The notions that valuing differences, the necessity of top team working, and the need to find forms of equitable 'functional balance' in organizations were more important to the new generation of directors than they had been to the last. There were signs of a new generation of managers, the baby boomers, making progress towards new ways of thinking about their organizations. The previous generation's 'Director as Hero' model, based on the cool, calculating logician with just a touch of the 'right stuff' – derring-do – was seen as insufficient. The 'Director as Conductor', of a complex series of teams, looked a more hopeful but still incomplete model. The 'Director as Developer' looked a much more positive approach – but a long way off.

The Development of Thinking as an Integrative Approach

The idea of the 'director as conductor', constantly monitoring and rebalancing the competing claims of the environment and the tribal fighting of the internal functions, seems increasingly helpful. It allows and encourages directors' thinking to transcend the internal and ultimately incestuous norms and values which organizations tend to encourage. It forces the reframing of easily and unthinkingly accepted ways of doing things by looking at the interactions between the functions of a business rather than within a single function. As most of us remain for the majority of our lives

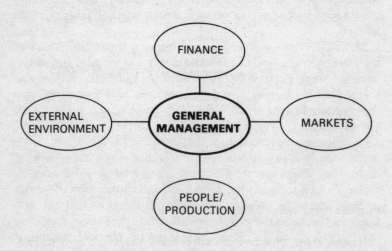

The traditional specialist areas

within our 'campus thinking' it is a helpful, if painful, process.

I was at a conference in 1980 with Professor John Morris[15] of the Manchester Business School. We were talking of advances in organizational thinking and he was speculating on the pictures that top managers hold of what it is they think they control – their domain. It was easy to draw the traditional view of that domain as it is so well known (see illustration on previous page). In most organizations emphasis is placed firmly on the vertical axis of finance/people/production with less interest on the horizontal aspects of markets and the external environment. Such organizations can easily become very comfortable in their niche and fail to respond to customers or the wider social and political trends.

To achieve responsiveness it is necessary to begin a series of reframings of the traditional view of the general managers' domain. If one rose a little above that view it is possible to get a clearer perspective of the elements necessary for the top managers to balance – to gain a more strategic view of their domain:

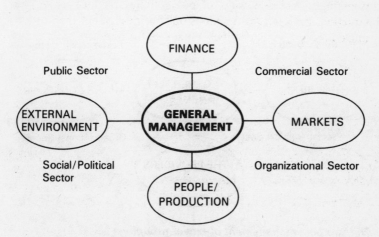

A transcending view of the traditional areas

Even so, most top managers will concede that their thinking and operations occur only in the right-hand quadrants, the traditional bases plus, perhaps, a little more market orientation. They will

avoid the public and social/political sectors if possible, and enter
them only with trepidation as it is felt that they are beyond their
'natural' domain. Yet they do accept, and often complain bitterly,
that more and more environmental, social, technological and
political pressures are pushing them towards the left-hand quadrants – whether they like it or not. In Britain this has been
illustrated by engineering companies such as Rolls Royce Aero-
engines, or Westland Helicopters, in the US by Chrysler and
Amtrak, in France by Framatome or St Gobain, in Italy by FIAT.
How can they begin to think and learn about these 'difficult',
'softer' and less-controllable sectors?

A helpful way of starting is to make the four co-ordinates more
identifiable, more personal, and less geared to the functional areas
of traditional business thinking. This allows a further stage of
reframing and the loosening of the old boundaries:

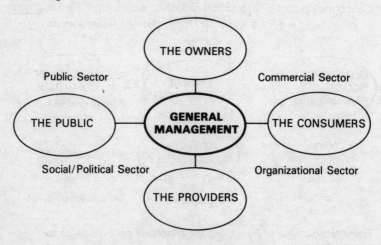

The strategic management of power groupings

Here we get a clearer view of the 'traditional' areas through the
use of the words 'owners', 'managers', 'providers', and 'consumers'. This makes strategic discussion easier as we are now out
of the conceptual shackles of the traditional specializations. It is
still difficult for many managers to cope with the public and

social/political sectors because this implies such a massive reinterpretation of their roles, and I shall return to these in greater depth later.

I have found that working through this three-step process does indeed release a director's thinking processes to operate on a much higher plane. It then seems a simple step to get agreement that such ultimate business goals as higher market share and a return on capital employed of over 30 per cent in any market are only achieved if the organization is competitively positioned to deliver quality to the consumer and the society which sustains it.

The model can then go through a fourth reframing to look at the issues of competitive quality which need to be balanced by the directors:

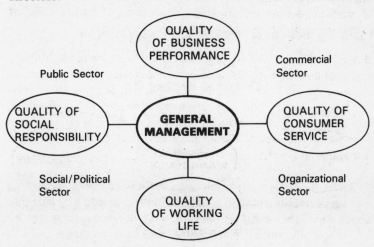

The strategic future? Balancing the organizational qualities for competitiveness

Behind all of this reframing lies the notion that it is the top manager's role to constantly monitor and adjust the strategic balance of an organization. Whilst much rhetoric is expended on the correctness of such an ideal, the blocking processes of uncertainty, lack of direction, and lack of personal development tend to cut in and ensure that the rhetoric rarely becomes behaviour –

at director level we tend not to do what we encourage others to do. In this way neither the organization nor the individual learns.

In the next section I will try to tease out the various levels of management needed to run an organization which is capable of continuously thinking and learning, and begin to design a process which can put that ideal into operation. Specifically I am interested in designing an organization which consciously and methodically looks upwards and outwards to its environment and its political and social relationships so that it can integrate these into its offerings to its consumers, yet also looks downwards to its internal productivity and efficiencies, and is capable of integrating the whole through a learning/planning process within an elegant organizational design.

Clarifying the Roles of Policy, Strategy, and Operations

'I don't think we have any directors who "are"; we're all "doing". The problem is what? The answer is that there are far too many of us doing the job below, because of a failure to delegate effectively. We have no end of directors, divisional directors, group directors, etc., all insisting on authorizing a myriad of minor operating detail over which they really should have no direct control.' Director, international construction company.

Whilst the 'balance' models used earlier are useful in clearing managers' minds about the validity and extent of the domains about which they need to think and take decisions, these models are essentially static. When using them the metaphor is of a director constantly seeking to return the organization to equilibrium – to maintain the stable state. Yet we know from many organizational and scientific studies that rapid manoeuvrability comes from forms of instability. It is no coincidence that modern fighter aircraft are designed to be inherently unstable, but highly manoeuvrable.

Few organizations can assume today that their 'normal' state is static and only reactive to environmental change. The external environment is dynamic, uncertain, and constantly changing as thousands of sectoral, national and international pressures react within it. To cope with such dynamism it is necessary to adopt the notion of 'proactivity', rather than reactivity, then to separate the key hierarchical managerial roles in the organization, ensure that people are properly trained and developed to play those roles competently, and then have a robust process for integrating them.

Often directors need to be reassured that it is scientifically 'respectable' to work with uncertainty before they will apply it to recognizable organizational problems. My physicist colleagues tell me that in many ways the frontiers of their science are now akin to fine art, with notions of 'elegance', 'quarks', 'weak forces', 'strangeness', etc. They refer to the influence in the 1920s of Godel's Theorem in the field of mathematics, and Heisenberg's uncertainty principle in philosophy – that the very act of observing changes both the object being observed and the observer. Such ideas have been translated into organizational terms by writers like Schon,[16] Toffler,[17] Naisbitt,[18] Drucker,[19] etc. From them all comes the notion that it is indeed respectable to think that the only thing of which we can be certain is that we are uncertain.

Back in the organization it is essential to identify a hierarchy of thinking roles for its members. There can be problems because the words used in the policy and strategy levels of business can confuse the issue. 'Strategy' is viewed by many managers as the apex of the thinking hierarchy. I believe that this is fundamentally wrong, and potentially dangerous to organizational survival.

It is significant to me that the policy/strategy/tactics hierarchy of organizing large numbers of people for specific ends has remained in constant use throughout recorded history. The ancient Chinese used such ideas five thousand years ago. In Europe the Greeks were using them three thousand years ago. They have served the Romans, Celts, and medieval Europeans as a model for warfare. Since the Renaissance they have been used for both warfare and the government of institutions. With the rise of industrial corporations they have been adopted by the modern world because they still form a well-tested, functional framework within which managers can work effectively.

Let me explain them in terms of the hierarchy of managerial thinking.

'Policy' is the highest level of the organizational thinking hierarchy and refers to 'political sagacity; prudence; skill or consideration of expediency in the conduct of public affairs; statecraft; or diplomacy; in a bad sense – political cunning'.[20] It has two branches from its Graeco-Latin root. The first concerns civil administration and government. The second, and less important to this argument, concerns the adjectives 'polished' and 'refined' which later became modified to mean cleanliness or neatness. In modern English the idea of policy has developed as a combination of wise, sophisticated, and tidy governance, coupled with the definition of the boundaries within which members of a society may exercise their liberties. I argue that the prime job of the direction-givers is to define policy for their organization, i.e. to give the basic rules within which others can plan the allocation of resources and tactics to achieve these broad objectives. If top managers are to become true policy-makers they need a conscious and rigorous programme of self-development to raise their consciousness, and develop appropriate attitudes, knowledge and skills. It is hardly surprising that many newcomers are intimidated by such expectations and opt for a low-level compromise which relies more on exerting their top managerial rights and less on the exercise of their direction-giving duties.

A 'strategist' is one versed in strategy. The Graeco-Latin root denotes a commander-in-chief, or a chief magistrate in Athens or the Achaen League. 'Strategy' comes into English from its classical roots through French to mean the 'command of a general, or generalship. The art of projecting and directing the larger military movements and operations of a campaign – usually distinguished from "tactics" which is the art of handling forces in battle, or in the immediate presence of the enemy'.

This fits perfectly my use of the term 'strategy' and 'tactics' or operations. The essence of the strategist is managing the conjunction of the political world, or 'polity', with the more day-to-day routines of tactics, and trying to keep them sufficiently in balance without allowing ossification. It is, therefore, essential for a director to have the ability to rise above the daily and weekly tactical detail so that he or she can project and direct the business's campaigns. But coping with politicians, pressure groups, and taking overviews are not the normal domains of top managers, especially those promoted from the ranks of the tacticians.

It seems that a developmental process is needed most here. It needs to encourage understanding and learning about the direction-giving duties and responsibilities which the wise policy-maker and strategist accepts.

The hierarchy I have described now looks like this:

POLICY

STRATEGY

OPERATIONS (tactics)

but this is still too static a notion to cope with a dynamic environment. One needs to add some movement to it, to begin to design interactions between the different levels so that each may learn from the others.

The essence of this part of my argument is, I hope, becoming clear – too many top management decisions are taken at too low a hierarchical level. There is a tendency in organizations around the world for directors to take too many decisions at the operational level, and too few at the policy and strategy levels. I believe that it is the duty of top managers to reverse this tendency and consciously to withdraw themselves from the 'hands on' comfort of day-to-day operations.

To make the change a two-level approach needs to be taken. At the personal level it is necessary to develop an understanding in the directors of the importance of their exercising their proper organizational role, learning to feel comfortable with that role, and arranging their priorities, particularly time, in a manner that reflects these as legitimate and necessary.

At an organizational level it is necessary to structure businesses so that the planning and decision-taking levels of policy, strategy and operations are defined clearly and integrated within a system so that people at each level of the hierarchy can understand and value the activities of the others. To develop this it is essential to consciously design 'organizations that learn'.

Developing Organizations That Learn

We know already from our review of second-order change and double-loop learning that a static and top-down approach will not allow sufficient feedback for an organization to learn. The three-level hierarchy is necessary but not sufficient. What is needed is a two-way flow of information so that directions can be given, and the operational consequences checked and adjusted, through a strategic integration mechanism (see illustration below). Unfortunately, most organizations have no such mechanism for doing this on a systematic basis. Interestingly, some Japanese companies claim to have been influenced in their organizational design by the work of Williamson, the inventor of the Quad amplifier, on multiple feedback loops.

When this dynamic information flow is added to the hierarchy, another reframing can occur. This different perspective places the direction-giver firmly astride the boundary between the organization and the outside world (see illustration opposite). Straddling this divide

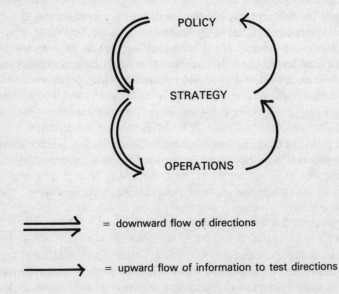

POLICY

STRATEGY

OPERATIONS

$\Longrightarrow$ = downward flow of directions

$\longrightarrow$ = upward flow of information to test directions

Information flows in a learning organization

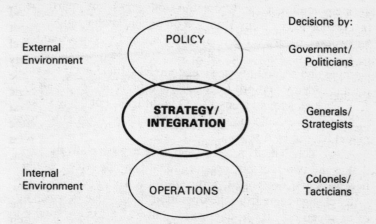

The hierarchy of direction-giving in a healthy organization

between the internal and external worlds of an organization is, for me, the definition of 'strategic thinking'.

It is this last version of the hierarchy which I will use to try to integrate and synthesize the content of my argument so far into a model of what constitutes a healthy learning organization.

The Learning Organization Model

It will come as no surprise now that the performance specification I have for the learning organization has certain characteristics:

1. A three-level hierarchy of policy/strategy/operations

2. A double loop of learning which allows multiple feedback from information flows, direction-giving, and the monitoring of changes in the external and internal environments

3. A means of processing and integrating these information flows by positioning the direction-givers at the centre of the organization's learning

Reflections and Concepts

In January 1980 I was at an Association of Teachers of Management conference at Templeton College, Oxford, participating in a session led by Tony Hodgson on organizational models.[21] We had worked before at Ellerman Lines and had kicked around some design ideas. Tony was, like me, interested in double-loop learning and second-order change models. I had been fascinated for a decade by Stafford Beer's elegant thesis on *The Brain of the Firm*[22] which I found compulsive but difficult, not being schooled in neurology or cybernetics. We were looking for a more robust model for use by directors.

As we debated, it became clear that it was relatively easy to define the two loops of organizational learning which would be necessary and, we hoped, sufficient for a workable model. First-order change came from the operations loop – one in which most of us spend our day-to-day working lives. This is essentially the process of doing 'more of' or 'less of' already established routines. Its rhythm is ritualistic and routine, with its rare drama being dependent on deviations from agreed plans. To achieve smooth running in the operations loop, organizations have developed specific control systems and set levels of performance by which to judge their success:

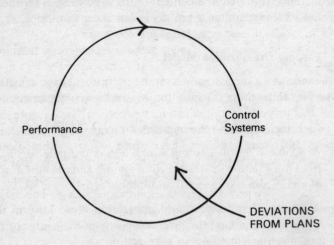

Performance

Control Systems

DEVIATIONS FROM PLANS

The basis of the operations loop of learning

This is the world in which most working people have found their position of psychological comfort. This is despite what they say about the turbulent effects of the Pythonesque foot which irregularly crashes out of the organizational sky, labelled 'Deviations From Plans', or about their doubts about the competence of the direction-givers. People can have some fun doing 'more of'/'less of' work. It can give changes of pace and some immediate drama. We know that this is psychologically necessary because in a well-run organization managers will add the drama themselves if they feel bored – by holding back on a project's start time to see if it can still be completed within the given time; by setting very high targets; by reducing manning levels, etc. – rather than let the system grind on quietly. A classic example in literature is the ever-increasing number of bombing missions needed to be completed before being withdrawn from the front line, described in *Catch-22*.[23]

Research shows that the north Europeans, specifically the British, Irish, Swedes, and Danes, are more prone, as a national grouping, to this than, say, the Americans or Australians. The Germans, Swiss, or French will resist much longer the need to add drama to a well-oiled machine. But ultimately we all like to stretch ourselves, and to test our competence through self-imposed constraints. There seems to be a Law of Human Cussedness which cuts in if things are too quiet.

We know that first-order change alone does not allow learning, except at the most mundane level. It is much closer to innate signal-response mechanisms. Reframing, by getting a better perspective through monitoring the external environment, rising above the immediate organizational problems, and identifying the wider issues, allows second-order change and, therefore, learning. But going into that wider world is less psychologically attractive for many directors. However, even they agree that the need to monitor environmental changes, and give subsequent direction, are key processes for a competent director. The major problem is, they tell me regularly, there is so little logic in the outside world that when the Pythonesque foot crashes into this loop they often feel helpless to take action.

Neither of these loops is sufficient in itself to demonstrate a learning organization, so one needs to design an integrative mechanism which acts as the central processor, the cerebral cortex of the organization, which brings together the information

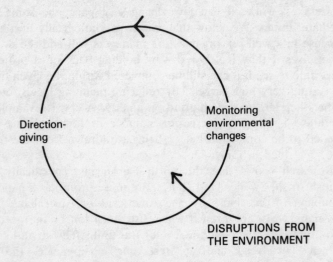

The basis of the policy loop of learning

flows, synthesizes them, and allows learning and development through the adaptation to change of the whole. The directors are literally central to this process – they are the integrators. The most apt metaphor I found for this was of the directors' role being the "business brain". I have used this in my model of the learning organization. It is a personal view and I should stress that it is not used in precisely the same way as Stafford Beer.

So now we have a model of the learning organization which looks as shown opposite.

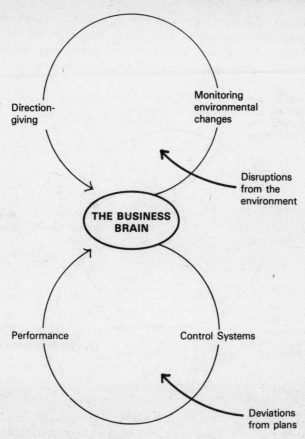

The learning organization model

Since 1980 I have been working with this model in many organizations around the world and have found it useful in helping directors understand the dimensions of their role. It seems to be powerfully memorable and capable of explaining to people at all levels of an organization what their duties, and rights, are within a business which is striving to increase its rate of learning so that it can survive and develop.

In talking with directors, the model can be viewed from different perspectives. In terms of the three-level hierarchy of organizational roles it can be seen as illustrated on p. 80.

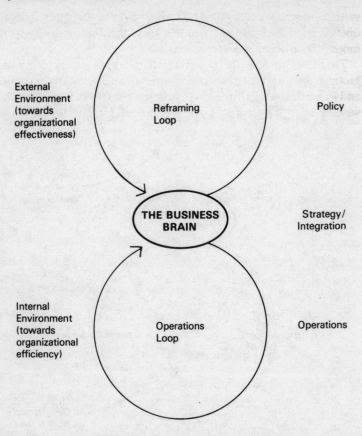

The learning organization and the three-level hierarchy

Such a perspective can open up the debate on where the managerial levels of an organization are best deployed and, most importantly, how they will deal with the boundaries between the different levels of the hierarchy. Such 'boundary management' issues are often avoided in organizations. The learning organization model highlights these issues. How do we manage the external/internal environmental boundaries? How does the operational side cope with policy and strategy? How does the total system integrate and synthesize? How will the directors delegate operations to their managers so that they, the directors, may spend more time on policy and integration issues?

The model has one other important characteristic. In a session with a group at the Institute of Directors it received an enthusiastic reception and we worked on clarifying some of the issues it raised. So much so that we developed, only half-jokingly, a 'Manifesto for Directors':

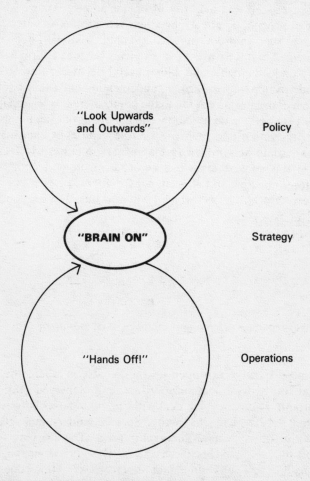

The 'Manifesto for Directors' of a learning organization

The learning organization model is still being refined. But it has held good for some six years in front of over a thousand directors. The ideas and processes behind it have worked well for over twenty years. It seems simple, given the luxury of 20/20 hindsight, so directors often react by saying, 'Well, we knew that . . . really'. In one sense this is true – the model is a representation of a basic human process.

However, the vast majority of organizations I know, whether public or private, do not arrange their activities to operate in such a clearcut way. In producing such a simplified model I hope that I have helped in three ways. First, by giving the idea a form which is readily understandable and allows useful debate to flow from it. Second, by making explicit a fundamental, but often avoided, problem of organizational life to the point where it is legitimate for directors to say 'we do not know enough about this' and to ask for help with getting into their proper role. Third, by showing that there are some well-proven developmental processes which can be used in this context to help generate competent directors and, therefore, effective and efficient organizations.

It is to this third aspect which I will now turn in the second part of the book.

Part Two

EXPERIMENTS AND ACTION

Section One
How Do We Get There?

This section is rather different from the preceding three. It contains a synopsis of maps, tools, and processes which have proved effective in helping to develop both the thinking and behaviour necessary to take up the roles outlined in the learning organization model. Most have been well-proven over the last two decades. Some are newer, but tested. [One of the joys of editing this Fontana series has been to have the luxury of commissioning unpublished work.] It is significant to me that all of the new work I have wanted to commission existed already in the authors' researches and practice, but had been perceived as 'not quite right' by the management education institutions. It is particularly significant to me that much of this new material is in the managerial thinking, strategy, and policy areas. It does seem that a sea change is occurring in Britain and that the notions that have been just below the surface are finding that their time seems to have come. They are surfacing as the directors of industry, government, social services, community services, charities, local groups, etc. are beginning to ask fundamental questions about the nature and processes of our organizations, and the qualities necessary in the people who run them. The good news is that the tools are ready and waiting to be used if people can grasp why they are necessary.

Developing the Conditions for Organizational Learning

A model much used, and sometimes abused, in management circles is Kolb's learning cycle (see illustration on next page).[24] It is based on the notion that learning is a cyclical process which needs to contain elements of each quadrant of the cycle before learning is possible. The key is to strike the personal balance with which we feel comfortable.[25]

My experience with directors has shown that, first, they tend to shy away from the reflection quadrant. The process of sitting back,

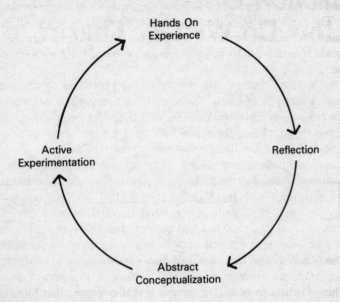

Kolb's learning cycle

observing what is happening, and testing this against what is meant to be happening does not come easily to them. Second, they tend to be very strong on active experimentation and love setting out on new projects and ventures. We know from other researches, referred to later, that they rarely like completing these tasks as they prefer to get involved in yet more new projects. Third, they fall into two distinct camps on the vertical axis – those that love to conceptualize and verbalize their worlds (but are not so keen on hands-on experience) and those who love to have their hands on the day-to-day levers of operational power and get quite put out if they are asked to look up and think in more abstract ways.

My experience is that there is little correlation between learning style and the industrial sector, but that there does seem to be a correlation with functional specialization – hands-on experience seems more comfortable with personnel, engineers, production, and accountants; active experimentation with marketing, projects, and lawyers. However, this is for the moment purely speculative.

The tendency for directors to reject reflection triggered in my mind the action learning experiences of managers around the world. Initially, their most common model of learning seemed to be:

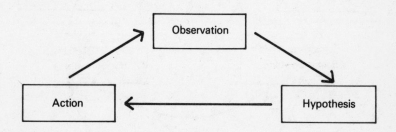

The action-fixated non-learning cycle

This resulted in a lot of action inside organizations, and if it didn't work the first time the managers went into a 'more of' mode and tried harder. This led quickly to their becoming comfortable with the idea that if they had a problem it was better to be seen to do something rather than stop and think. The value seemed to be that it was better to work harder than to work smarter. It seems to me that effective managers tend to pause to reflect, in my terms 'reframe', before they take action. The act of pausing, however momentarily, allows a more relaxed and accurate approach, whether the topic be sport or management. Managers who do reflect seem to do so in two distinct phases. First, after an observation which excites their curiosity. Second, after putting forward a hypothesis for testing so that it may be debated and constructively criticized. This latter, action learning, process can be shown as illustrated on p. 88. This is much closer to a true scientific process. It is significant that action learning 'sets' (self-help groups) are designed so that participants discuss observations, constructively criticize hypotheses, and give support to their 'comrades in adversity' whilst action and reaction to their

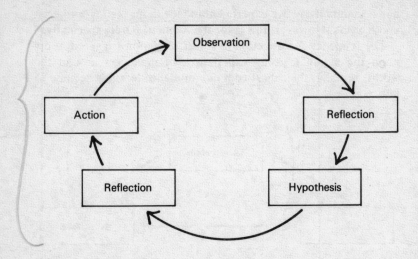

The action learning cycle

plans take place in the organization. Hence the argument that it is better to strive to be an 'action learner' than an action-fixated manager. My experience is that this is as valid for directors. Indeed it is highly beneficial for developing directors to become reflective, less hands-on, less abstract, and less isolated in their direction-giving.

Recent work by Max Boisot[26] also uses the metaphor of a learning cycle. But rather than focus on the learning processes of an individual he is interested in how organizations learn. He identifies two crucial axes with which to describe the process of organizational knowledge creation and distribution – codification and diffusion.

'Codification' is the psychological process by which an idea is brought in from the external world, worked on by people in the organization, and turned into some form of intellectual property which it is possible to sell back to the outside world.

'Diffusion' is an essentially sociological process through which the codified knowledge can be transmitted to another interested party. The form of diffusion will be culturally determined by both parties, often on national, political, or religious lines. Boisot describes the organizational learning cycle as shown opposite.

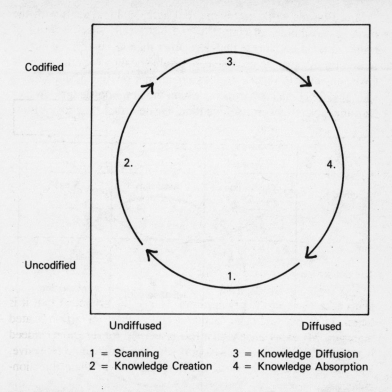

Boisot's four phases of new knowledge flows

For a business the codification axis is involved in investment in learning costs (not a normal budget item in such terms), whilst the diffusion axis is about communication costs (a normal budget item). Moving from uncodified knowledge (what is held in the hands and minds of researchers and engineers) and transforming it into codified knowledge (in software programs, manuals, specifications, etc.) is a complex process of organizational psychology. Taking undiffused knowledge (the innovations, breakthroughs, and commercial secrets of the firm) and selling them into the world through culturally acceptable trade forms is a delicate political and anthropological process.

Experiments and Action

Max Boisot's work on 'managerial anthropology' deals with the exciting possibilities of culturally and historically specific forms of trade, so I will not pursue that here other than to say this is a further reason for directors to become comfortable dealing with the external environment. However, Boisot's comments on the positioning of specialist functional departments within the new knowledge flows, or learning cycle, are worthy of mention. He describes the process thus:

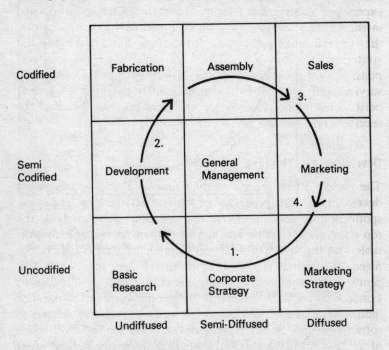

The position of specialist departments in Boisot's learning cycle

Again, it is significant that general management, the 'direction-givers' in my terms, are centrally situated in the model and seem to follow the director-as-conductor and director-as-developer ideas. Using my three-level hierarchy and the learning organization model one can see the reframing loop as the right-hand sections, the operations loop as the left-hand sections, with strategy and integration being in the central sections.

I hope that these brief remarks on the learning process will, when linked with the comments on intellectual property rights in Section 3 of Part 1, show that learning is fundamental to the survival of a business and, therefore, its directing and managing processes. In these terms learning is much too important to be left as the province of the personnel or, even worse, the training departments. It is the key function of top managers. In my experience learning and training are often diametrically opposed in their values and processes. Taken seriously, learning affects the organizational structure, processes, and developmental strategies of a business. Therefore, it must be the key responsibility of the directors if they are to protect the continuing survival and growth of their business. They neglect it at their peril, as many of the companies which end up in the hands of the receivers find out too late.

Developing the Thinking Processes

The middle 1980s are an exciting time in British management development. The processes of managerial thinking are being spotlighted as needing drastic re-evaluation, particularly at the top management level. The need for them to become comfortable with the 'hands off/brain on' approach is increasingly recognized as essential if they are to survive into the twenty-first century. Whether one is facing the 'Big Bang' in the City of London, coping with the effects of automation on a smokestack industry, or pondering on how to motivate creative people in software writing or design, it is obvious that the old-style 'more of' or 'less of' behaviour and thought patterns are not sufficient to cope with the rate of change. The problem is how does one do anything about it?

Luckily two types of tool exist to help. First, the notion of brief therapy applied to role change for directors. If one subscribes to the notion of the policy/strategy/operations hierarchy and the model of organizational learning, then it is relatively easy to see that the deployment of directors' time[27] needs to achieve three ends:

1. To release their 'hands-on' behaviour so that they have time to think.

2. To set up systems for 'looking upwards and outwards' so that they have the ability usefully to reframe current organizational problems.

3. To position themselves to act competently as the 'brain' function of the business, being the organizational cortex through which internal and external environmental messages are processed.

None of these comes easily. Getting a 'hands-on' specialist to devote time regularly to reading newspapers, watching TV, and debating micro, mega, and meta trends is an interesting process, even before one starts adding serious economic, political, technological, and social analysis, and that is before one starts to learn the integrative skills of organizational design and direction-giving.

But it can be done, and small, incremental, behavioural changes can have an impressive cumulative impact. Even acts as simple as reading a 'serious' newspaper before starting work each day (in its more advanced form this becomes being comfortable reading a newspaper at work) and then debating items of interest at coffee or lunch can have a liberating effect on directors. It begins to show both privately and publicly that it is legitimate for directors to take an interest in the outside world and to manage the boundary between the organization and that wider world by rising above the daily micro-political fights. We know that this is better done as a group development activity, rather than on an individual basis. Later in this section I will go deeper into this when I deal with 'Teams at the Top'.

Who Gets to the Top?

The issue of the selection of directors is often clouded in mystery and myth in business. Two obvious criteria form the breeding grounds for the widespread view of incompetence at the director level – the Peter Principle writ large. The first is 'having to serve one's time'. This assumes that the organization sees a directorship as a reward not for competence but often for 'not making a wrong move' over a long period. Such an approach can have meaning in a paternalistic organization, but it encourages risk-averse directors who will be dominated by the chairman, president, or chief executive. Yet direction-giving is all about taking risks – hopefully well-informed ones.

The second criterion often quoted is that the new director was chosen because he or she was 'our kind of person'. Whilst often said in a way that is complimentary – the top team is truly pleased to have such a person on board as they reflect accurately the values and behaviour for which the others stand – it can lead to similar problems of risk-averseness as the 'Buggin's turn' approach of the first. This second approach was fashionable in, for example, financial services groups during the 1960s and 1970s and was widely believed to be based on 'the old school tie' as the entry ticket. My own view is that such groups were wise enough to see that they would have to add new people, like computing and technological staff, who would not be from the same background so they spent time and considerable sums of money on developing social poise and acceptability in these newcomers. They would never be like the others but there would be a layer of lubrication which would help their integration.

'Country house' management schools grew fat on the profits of 'instilling the corporate ethos in our new directors' programmes, until around 1980 when colder winds blew. This does not apply only to the United Kingdom. In continental Europe and the USA all sorts of social tests and initiation rites are performed before one gets a director's chair. In the Far East matters tend to be rather different as the notion of business as an extension of the family structure makes matters simpler, and simultaneously much more complex.

There is a third, rather sad, group who become 'directors'. These seem to have all the disadvantages of the title and very few of the advantages. These are the folk who have a director job title 'because their job demands it'. They tend not to be members of the statutory board of directors. They are found in companies where the statutory companies have moved out of synchronization with their trading companies, and these 'directors' tend to be in the trading companies. They are also found in companies where a lot of foreign travel and negotiation are involved so 'they have to have the title or the customers would not do business with us'; and where the title was given, but none of the power, to keep someone in the company, for whatever reason. They are not in my terms direction-givers and tend to lead a more frustrating life than most managers in the organization.

These latter can have a very hard time of it. If you are a statutory director you can at least understand your legal position, and have some notion of what performing a competent job is about. Non-statutory directors often try to assume the direction-giving stance and are squashed regularly by the Pythonesque foot of, say, the Group or 'those across the pond', forcing them back into a line predetermined elsewhere. This is a frustrating position, part of which can be clarified by at least using the distinction between chief executive officers (usually statutory directors) and chief operating officers (often non-statutory 'directors') in their job titles.

But even then there is the issue of responsibility and liability. In some circumstances directors are thought to be legally liable for both the civil and criminal misdeeds of their business. Yet few seem aware of this when they accept the title. This is a messy area which needs resolving by the asking of discriminating questions before taking up the role. It is similar to the problems that professional practices, like architects, have experienced in the past. To reward, and hopefully retain, good people, 'associates' were declared whose names then appeared on the notepaper. They were not part of the Partnership Deed and did not reap the benefits of it. However, when hard times arose there were those who found that they were legally obliged to pay a proportion of the sometimes massive debts involved.

All things considered, the present lack of rigorous thought about the selection of future directors, and the legal structures within which they work, can seem a little depressing. However, all is not lost.

Some Ways Forward on Thinking

Britain is developing some creative tools for helping to resolve the present mess over the selection of directors. The noted British ability to absorb and enjoy ambiguity and uncertainty is working in its favour. This characteristic, noted in many anthropological works but strongly in Geert Hofstede's *Cultures Consequences*,[28] is part of the thought process necessary for adopting a design-based, creative approach to direction-giving. It can be released and developed quite rapidly once it is seen as legitimate, even laudable, in an organization to do so. This means that the powerbrokers at the chief executive, chairman, and owner levels have to be seen to encourage the process, otherwise one ends up with unthinking 'think-tanks' and odious 'skunk works'.

Two strong and creative notions have permeated almost invisibly, and with little publicity, British management education in the last decade. One is the previously mentioned pioneering work of Action Learning, where crucial organizational problems are taken as the vehicle for simultaneous manager and organizational development, thereby ensuring a cost-effective investment in the organization's human resources. Today no self-respecting practitioner would put in a developmental proposal which did not have at least an 'action plan' attached to it. In action learning terms this is near blasphemy as the idea is that the learning can only come through taking action, not by talking about it. However, the idea of action-based thought is beginning to root.

Second, the best-selling but undersung work of Tony Buzan, *Use Your Head*,[29] has percolated corporate thinking in a major way. His ways of recording ideas, rather than immediately evaluating them in a binary manner, are found in 'mind maps' all over the world and his simple, practical approach to thinking as a key activity has helped legitimize the idea across a wide spectrum of organizational life. He, along with others like Edward De Bono, have helped focus on the thinking process as a necessary building block for managers and, I would add, directors.

Thinking Intentions

To these earlier pioneers can be added the work of Jerry Rhodes and Sue Thame and their 'Thinking Intentions Profile'.[30] They grapple with a serious problem of scientific process and methodology. Curiously, we have not developed an accurate way of describing people's thinking intentions – what it is they are attempting when they set out to do something. There is no agreed vocabulary for so doing and the area has tended to be left alone as annoying but unimportant.

Jerry Rhodes, Sue Thame, and their fellow researchers aided by initial support from Philips, Eindhoven, seem to have made a breakthrough. Their six-part basic model of thinking intentions can be taken deeper into a twenty-three-character alphabet which allows a precise measurement of the combination and weightings given to a person's thinking intentions, and can be used to assess their effectiveness against the problem posed. I do not intend to go into the range of the Thinking Intentions Profile here. However, the basic six-part model is worthy of further mention as it has been helpful in clarifying some aspects of directorial thinking. The centre of the Thinking Intentions Profile (TIP) model is the idea that a person embarks on a thinking process with the intention of doing something. 'Do' is therefore the axis around which all re-volves. There are three major categories of thinking intentions:

Ideas

Information

Judgement

Each has two elements, labelled 'hard' and 'soft'. Hard ideas relate to ingenuity and the ability to innovate on existing ideas or artefacts. Soft ideas are essentially visionary in nature and tend to put together previously unconnected notions, derived from what Boisot would refer to as the 'diffused but uncodified' world. In that sense they are 'new' ideas. Hard information is precisely that. It is codified, recorded and measurable – the hard facts. Soft information involves the senses, what is really going on behind the hard facts, so it is concerned with the smell, feel, and taste of situations. Hard judgement is the rational, logical evaluation of the facts as presented. Soft judgement relies much more on the emotional weighting of values which could be viewed as essentially binary – 'right or wrong', 'good or bad', etc. The whole can be characterized by the following diagram:

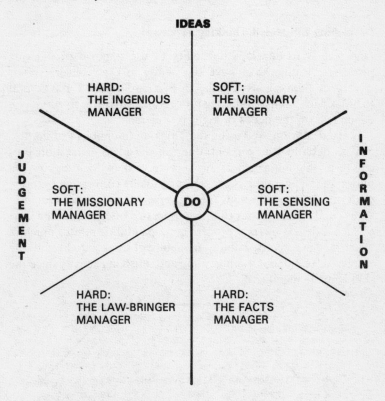

A basic model of the Thinking Intentions Profile

Whilst the research data is still being compiled, so that 'norms' can be derived for industry, the nation, age, sex, and other groupings, my experience using the TIP with directors tells me that most people have been taught the 'hard' areas as the 'right and only' ones for a 'good' manager. Their 'missionary' belief is that all managers should be of the unemotional, fact-orientated, ingenious, law-bringer stereotype. Organizational life rarely reinforces this view, yet they have not been taught to act on the other soft aspects – sensing, envisioning – which develop the rich emotional life of organizations. How can one begin to do that?

Developing Integrated Thinking Processes

One way is to develop the ability to use a range of thinking processes. Rather than have the ability to use 'convergent' or 'divergent' thinking, as described in Section 3 of Part 1, it is helpful to break such a binary thinking process and learn how to adopt one dependent on the needs of a given situation.

In its ideal form, and using the Thinking Intentions Profile, this can be described as concentrating on the ideas-generation processes in the initial stages of a project, then focusing on the information-generating processes, and finally converging onto the preferred solution through the judgemental processes. Our previous conditioning about thinking processes often makes the start of such a developmental process quite painful, it refutes much in which we have invested about the nature of what is 'right', but the results suggest that it is a liberating and satisfying activity once the skill is made manifest.

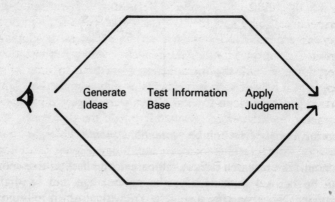

The integrated thinking process for directors

Another way is to concentrate on breaking the conceptual confines of the old technical-specialist boundaries and to develop a position in which directors can feel comfortable dealing with more general and integrated issues. Before moving on to speculation about the selection criteria of directors as individuals or team members, it is worth reinforcing the idea that to become effective, directors will have to drop much of the specialist training that took them so far in the organization and become more generalist, and integrative, in their direction-giving approach.

I am conscious of some irony here. Many directors have criticized people, such as senior civil servants, who have cultivated a more generalist approach. They are called 'dilettante', 'out of touch' and 'too generalist'. Yet they can rise above a technical problem, see the wider perspective, and integrate their thinking. All of these are admirable qualities which, if creativity is added, are essential for effective directors.

It seems that a balance needs to be struck within each director so that he or she can become comfortable with the specialist/ generalist role. The argument has been an issue in the diplomatic world for some time. US Ambassadress to the United Nations, Jeanne Kirkpatrick, makes the point of both valuing difference through the use of specialists and yet being able to integrate those specialisms: 'I do believe the periodic introduction of different kinds of specialist – for example the political scientist, which I am, or for that matter the political legislator – gives some fresh perspectives, some new ideas. I think that one of the pitfalls of very large bureaucracies is of a certain staleness developing, a certain lack of imagination, the tendency to the routinization of everything. I think the introduction from time to time of new people at relatively high levels helps us fight against that. Unlike certain past ages when foreign affairs were largely diplomatic in character, and therefore reasonably left to the diplomats, it has become a very different kind of activity in which diplomacy is only one tool. Foreign affairs today are multi-dimensional, including an economic dimension, a military dimension, and a cultural dimension with educational exchanges and communication and intelligence functions. There has to be a point in government which co-ordinates all of these perspectives on foreign affairs and diplomacy.'[31]

If we change the words 'foreign affairs' for direction-giving and 'government' for the company, then we have a useful statement of what a future board should be doing.

Some Possible Selection Measures for Directors

None of the rather crude stereotypes of directors mentioned so far is typical of everyone. It is the unique combination of characteristics, which instruments like TIP help measure, which need codifying and considering when selecting the top team. The range of measuring tools in psychology is now wide.

More importantly, it is possible to compare individual director scores with each other not just as an evaluation of those individuals but as a way of 'mapping' the human resources available within a top team. When this is done and the map derived, similarities can be noted and differences identified. Ashby's Law of Requisite Variety can be used to consider present and previous selection processes, and a healthier and more effective top team derived.

The process of mapping team differences and gaps, rather than focusing on individual scores, is an important psychological process to which I will return in the top teams part of this section. Here we can begin to consider an individual's characteristics when facing up to the turbulent and ambiguous world of direction-giving. There are now tests for assessing, for example:

Specialist and generalist preferences (particularly convergent and divergent thinking patterns)
The ability to tolerate and value differences
The ability to cope with uncertainty and ambiguity
The ability to tolerate three types of risk-taking (physical, emotional, and financial)
The ability to take an issue-based 'helicopter' view of problems

The interesting thing is that if one rejects binary thinking in the selection and assessment processes (they either pass, or they fail), and uses 'both/and' thinking, then it seems wise to concentrate on developing existing directors to achieve their maximum abilities, rather than using the 'surgical' approach by trying to replace anyone who does not already have the necessary capability. This may still not result in the sort of top team 'map' that would be ideal, but it would give a good picture of what capabilities already existed, who needed to be developed and how, and only then a description of the type of people needed to fill the gaps. This would allow a more 'holistic' view of the composition of the top team to be taken and lead to more accurate identification of effective potential directors. Moreover, it would help identify the sort of people not required (more of the same).

In one sense we are beginning to deal with the left and right hemispheres of the brain of the firm. In management education and consultancy we have spent some three decades developing the corporate brain as though it only had a left hemisphere (rational, logical, quantitatively-based). We seem now to be on the threshold of an era when more attention will be paid to the right hemisphere (emotional, creative, visual, sensing). The thinking processes mentioned briefly above should help greatly in this process towards what Jacqueline Wonder has described as 'whole brain thinking'.[32] However, it must be remembered that the brain is the ultimate integrator and does not operate in discrete sections. We should not design our top teams, or organizations, so to do.

Integrating the Technical With the People Side of Learning

An important part of developing the thinking processes of competent directors is getting them to handle the 'soft' areas of people and emotions as well as the 'hard' areas of analysis and judgement, and to believe that both are necessary to be effective.

The work of Bion[33] at the Tavistock Institute in the 1930s demonstrated clearly that any problem involving relationships had two components, both of which had to be managed simultaneously if the problem was to be successfully resolved. The first was the 'technical' aspect. This is the area where most professionals, including engineers, accountants, personnel, etc. have had their training focused. It is an area of comfort for most managers. The second, the 'social emotional' aspect, is rarely developed in management training. This seems particularly true of top managers

101

around the world. The social emotional aspect deals with the management of the emotional temperature of personal relationships. This can be daunting to top managers, even though they can grasp intellectually that getting people enthused, committed, and participating is theoretically part of their role. A helpful explanation of Bion's idea seems to be that the technical, or task, aspect is about getting the content side of a problem solved. The management of the social emotional aspect provides the film of lubrication which allows the technical mechanism to work. Without the social emotional side being consciously managed, the problem-solving process overheats and seizes up. Then nothing is solved.

One way of looking at this issue is to see the director's job as essentially an organizational problem-solving process. The inputs are technical, and social emotional. The need is to strike an appropriate balance between the two inputs so that the problem-solving is effective. This can be described as:

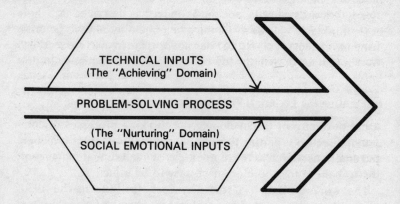

TECHNICAL INPUTS
(The "Achieving" Domain)

PROBLEM-SOLVING PROCESS

(The "Nurturing" Domain)
SOCIAL EMOTIONAL INPUTS

Two inputs to the problem-solving process

There seems to be an almost global notion of top management in which hard men, rarely women, do logical things in a tough-minded way, and if the employees don't like it they can lump it. My observations of top teams shows me that commonly the level of creativity, and creating visions of the future, is low, as is being seen to care for people, the management of the social emotional area.

Does this matter? Is this not yet another potential appeal by wimps for 'soft' (in the pejorative sense) managers? No. If one believes that the only source of intellectual property development is learning, then the only resource for learning in a competitive world is the workforce one employs. If employees are misdirected and mismanaged in the social emotional aspect of the learning process, rather than just the personnel terms and conditions sense, then they will become disruptive, unproductive, block learning, and/or leave. Anyone who has managed a software or design department will know how easy it is to kill learning and create a subversive subculture.

Most of an organization's intellectual property will be in a semi-codified or uncodified state; it is held in the heads and hands of the members, so mismanagement in this area leads to highly ineffective businesses. Organizational learning is an investment in human capital that is intangible and so never shows up on a company's balance sheet until a successful takeover bid is made. Ironically, it is then registered as 'good will'.

It is useful to remember that the English word 'manager' derives from two distinct roots. In the sixteen century it enters the language from the Italian '*maneggiare*' – one who breaks horses – the true macho-manager, the Achiever. In the eighteenth century it is separately derived from the French '*menager*' – the domestic economy of a household or kitchen – the nurturing manager notion. The English term 'manager' should, therefore, incorporate both. It is sad that at present it rarely does in practice. If the future of business is dependent on learning then we will have to learn how to incorporate them to survive.

Developing Top Teams

Some specific issues need addressing before we can go deeply into the top team development process. First, there is a need to demonstrate that an organization will operate effectively only if it is seen as a series of co-operating teams working across the horizontal and vertical groupings within the business. It is important to learn how to strike a balance between the West's rampant individualism, or selfishness, and the Orient's need for 'extended family' work teams. This balance is needed particularly at the top of an organization. It is patently absurd to select a project group in which one discipline, or personality, is so dominant that the whole is out of balance. It will not be able to deliver to the marketplace consistent quality in all aspects to satisfy its clients. Yet it happens often. It is even more absurd to select a top team dominated by such a strong personality or discipline that the other members cannot exercise their true roles of integration and direction-giving. Yet this, too, happens with depressing regularity.

The notion of the 'strong man' who will lead everyone at all times is pervasive in the literature and folklore of management. But there are few examples that stand the test of time in a complex business. As the Center for Creative Leadership, Greensboro, and other studies seem to show, early perceived initial success is 'derailed' by the inability of the top manager to get the whole organizational system up and learning continuously. The 'power culture' of the charismatic leader can work wonders in the short term but can kill a business in the medium to long term. In many ways the problem can be traced back to who selects and develops directors, particularly chief executives. It is very tempting to a president, chairman, or group managing director to put in a 'hard' individual as chief executive. This can lead to encouraging early results, until the system strikes back. Then we get into the 'guaranteed failure' cycle. He fails and is replaced two or three years after his appointment and the process is repeated. The Bourbons have arrived.

In the short term nearly any profit-and-loss account and balance sheet can be interpreted 'creatively' to show that things are looking better. But they cannot be manipulated constantly without finally having to reframe the problem. In doing so one needs to take a longer view, and add a lot of different brains to the problem. This is where the top team can come into its own – provided that it comprises very different people who nevertheless respect each other. Not knowing the others' specialisms can then be a positive advantage. Action learning is strong on the use of 'intelligent naivety' to open up intractable problems. Someone with intelligence, but no specialist knowledge, can and should ask fundamental, or discriminating, questions of the experts. These are precisely the questions that the experts assume as given by top management before they start their work. To develop such a system needs the top team to see itself as a debating and criticizing forum of equals who frame their questions in terms of the total business. Here it pays not to pursue specialist ends, or tell other specialists how to do their jobs. It pays most of all to be a little naive about the technical issues, to pause and maintain the ability to reflect, so that you are not fooled by the ever-present techno-speak.

To achieve better perspectives and the creative use of the differences embodied in a top team on a regular basis it seems that we are looking for top managers, or, even better, management teams, who are strong at balancing both achievement (task-directed behaviour) and nurturing (people-directed behaviour). To develop a process for achieving this it is necessary to attack the image of the single, macho-manager, capable of coping with all problems by a predetermined idea of what constitutes the right answer and the right management style. This approach can lead to a temporary feeling of comfort-through-certainty but it is not a thinking and learning process related to each problem and its context. Using the macho-manager approach is increasingly ineffective because it misses the subtleties of specific situations and, by so doing, reduces the chances of the others involved committing themselves to the action advocated. In organizations where the educational quality of the workforce is rising rapidly this is a particularly foolish approach.

The Failings of Top Teams

John Argenti in his book *Corporate Collapse: Causes and Symptoms*[34] has described six symptoms of collapse which have existed in whole or part in all the organizations he investigated:

1. One-man rule

2. A non-participating board

3. An unbalanced top team

4. A lack of management depth

5. A weak finance function

6. A combined chairman and chief executive role

This interested me, particularly as the highly acclaimed work of Cork Gully and Company (often referred to as the 'Official Receivers') showed great similarities with their analyses of the businesses they had taken into receivership, some of them world names, and their causes of failure:

1. An autocratic chief executive – who does not listen to colleagues or advisers and goes for growth only

2. Unbalanced boards – too much similarity on a board is dangerous, especially with engineers, and particularly when they lack financial expertise

3. Lack of management information systems – little testing against the current economic climate

In all these conditions Cork Gully make the point that 'mistakes are made because the climate for making mistakes exists'.[35]

The last point rang true. In creating boards in their own image, by encouraging conformity, by limiting differences and, therefore, the opportunities for creativity, by encouraging 'groupthink' and its associated feeling of invulnerability and moral superiority, and by blocking debate, the 'accident-prone board' is created.

The idea that debate is missing in the non-participating board intrigued me as there seems now to be a counter-culture emerging, two aspects of which are of special interest.

First, action learning 'sets' – typically four to six people meeting on a regular basis to tackle simultaneously both organizational and personal development problems – use a rigorous process of constructive criticism and support. They encourage debate about technical issues (the 'achieving' domain), but they also see the participants as 'comrades in adversity' and spend time supporting and encouraging each other (the 'nurturing' domain). In this way tasks get finished, individuals are developed personally, and strong teams can be built. This seems a useful model for the development of boards.

In his work on 'groupthink'[36] Irving Janis compares John F. Kennedy's leadership style during two major crises of his administration. During the Bay of Pigs fiasco, Kennedy took control of all meetings, evaluated heavily the inputs of his staff, and generally subscribed to one-man rule. The result is still an embarrassment to the American people. During the Cuban missile crisis, a short time later, Kennedy selected a crisis-control team he could trust, then encouraged open debate, ensured that he was not present at all meetings so that the team would have to take responsibility for progressing the problem, held back on the early evaluation of inputs, and nurtured the learning of his team. The result went a long way to ensuring that the world was not plunged into nuclear war.

The idea of the board as the open debating chamber of an organization is often considered weird and unachievable by directors when they first encounter it. Objections are raised that the board is really a legal device to look after shareholders' interests, or an auditing mechanism responsible to the owners for its actions. This is true. But where then is the brain of the firm? Where will the intellectual process of integration, synthesis, and debate rather than rhetoric take place? The truth is that in many organizations it does not happen, except at odd moments in the mind of the president, chairman, or managing director. To get it to happen in a board it is crucial to be able to run such debates as a meeting of equals. This can cause social problems for a top team in the early stages of such a process. It will already have a power structure, a pecking order, which will tend to freeze out, or deliberately under-value, the inputs of the others. Learning to recognize and block this reaction is essential to board development. Learning to value the inputs, which are often disconcerting or carry bad news, is a necessary skill for directors. It is a precondition of an effective top team. Actions taken from such debate are more rooted in creative reality than the actions of any single, macho chief executive.

The second noteworthy aspect of the counter-culture is the growing use of non-executive directors (NEDs)[37] on boards. When the original Companies Acts were proclaimed, NEDs were seen as a necessary balance to ensure that what were essentially family-dominated businesses gave some acknowledgement to the outside world and the interests of non-family shareholders. Over the years the role of many NEDs was played down, or lost completely. They were either absorbed in the 'more of the same' selection processes, or they were dropped as statutory boards went out of synchronization with the trading companies in the larger industrial groups – and no one knew quite what a 'director' was meant to do.

Complacency, virtual incest, and a lack of debate between directors led to 'brainless businesses', or at best lobotomized organizations, whose neural connections left a lot to be desired. The board was characterized by organizational wits as the 'black hole' which absorbed all known creative talent, neutralized it, and from which no human being ever emerged. The world recession of the early 1980s has shaken that earlier complacency and feeling of invulnerability. Outsiders with different ideas, different experiences, and the ability to debate and integrate – to ask discriminating questions before taking action – are slowly being invited onto boards to help their learning processes. Of special hope is the relatively easy use of NEDs by the newer, high-tech companies which are aware of their restricted disciplinary and business experience base.

Looking back at the failed boards of companies in the major industries – steel, aero-engines, cars, and now electronics – it does seem that Ashby's Law of Requisite Variety is something to contemplate. At first it is not comfortable for a board to value and manage such differences. But it is essential for survival in a changing world. It helps transcend the war cries of failing boards, war cries such as 'not invented here', 'not our class of customer', 'we prefer not to do business with such people', or 'our product sells itself'. The problem with brainless businesses is that they often take a long time to die, more than a decade, and dealing with the wasting disease of lack of thought at the top is seen as no one's responsibility.

Dealing with it takes time. In a way it is like learning a form of organizational judo where you learn to use the power of the opposition and the environment to conserve your slim energies and still win. It is easy to forget to value differences in the turmoil of day-to-day managing. When my clients say this I have to agree. But what, I ask, are you as a director doing dabbling in day-to-day tactics? I thought you were in top management? The typical response is, 'Yes, but . . .' followed by a desperate post-rationalization about how this time the situation was different. It does take great self-discipline to learn to delegate to staff when you know that you can do the job better than them – after all you have had more experience . . . But that is why you were appointed a director.

Let's start again. It is an act of self-development to face up to becoming a more generalist, more cerebral, more integrative, less action-fixated director. It is highly developmental for all parties to undertake a system of coaching subordinates to bring them on to take over your old job. A special skill is to allow them to make mistakes without your intervening. Your temperature may rise, your heart bleed, and your hands ache to get hold of the problem, but your subordinates have to learn as well. There is an old nautical reference to the first time the first mate attempts to dock the ship – 'The captain must bite his tongue until it bleeds'.

I use an assessment test to check a director's inclination to delegate and regularly find depressing scores from people who 'know' they should be delegating, but find it hard to break the ingrained behaviour of years. It may well be that future board members will be given contracts for, say, five-year periods after which a rigorous assessment of their directorial effectiveness will determine their right to continue to sit on the board.

The Composition of Teams

Meredith Belbin's excellent work *Management Teams: Why They Succeed or Fail*[38] is worth study in relation to the design of top teams. It is not my intention to make a detailed analysis of Belbin's book here. However, I will mention some aspects I have found helpful when working with directors. He lists eight types of people who need to be present in an effective management team (see table on next page). Belbin's ideas people are called 'plants' because his otherwise good teams were usually deficient in ideas and needed to be 'planted' with such people. There does seem to be as much of a problem generating high-quality ideas with top teams as with any other teams. The management and valuing of ideas people is also a problem and new ways are being developed to try and maintain their use to the top team rather than be ground down

Useful people to have in teams

Type	Typical Features	Positive Qualities	Allowable Weakness
Company Worker	Conservative, dutiful, predictable	Organizing ability, practical common sense, hard-working, self-discipline	Lack of flexibility, unresponsiveness to unproven ideas
Chairman	Calm, self-confident, controlled	A capacity for treating and welcoming all potential contributors on their merits and without prejudice. A strong sense of objectives	No more than ordinary in terms of intellect or creative ability
Shaper	Highly strung, outgoing, dynamic	Drive and a readiness to challenge inertia, ineffectiveness, complacency or self-deception	Proneness to provocation, irritation and impatience
Plant	Individualistic, serious-minded, unorthodox	Genius, imagination, intellect, knowledge	Up in the clouds, inclined to disregard practical details or protocol
Resource Investigator	Extroverted, enthusiastic, curious	A capacity for contacting people and exploring anything new. An ability to respond to challenge	Liable to lose interest once the initial fascination has passed
Monitor/ Evaluator	Sober, unemotional, prudent	Judgement, discretion, hard-headedness	Lacks inspiration or the ability to motivate others
Team Worker	Socially orientated, rather mild, sensitive	An ability to respond to people and to situations, and to promote team spirit	Indecisiveness at moments of crisis
Completer/ Finisher	Painstaking, orderly, conscientious, anxious	A capacity for follow-through. Perfectionism	A tendency to worry about small things. A reluctance to 'let go'

Reprinted by permission of William Heinemann Ltd.

by it. Top teams are usually much more comfortable with 'second-hand ideas', that is ideas which happen through the resource investigator, or 'fixer' – the role of knowing the people who can make things happen for you.

The power struggles in a team are usually fought out between the holders of high 'shaper' and 'chairman' scores. The chairman is the open, public role of seeing balance and fair play in the team, and is not the same as having the formal title of 'chairman'. The shaper is the unofficial chairman, trying to shape discussion his or her way without necessarily being open about it. This is a common organizational fight which can be worked on quite easily using brief therapy processes.

I have found a high number of monitor/evaluator scores in the top teams with which I have dealt, which suggests that they are not very open to ideas or debate. I have found almost no completer/finishers! This would fit the idea of the action-fixated ex-perimenters who do not really want to know what happens and how it can be refined, but get their kicks out of setting up the action in the first place, and then intervening, apparently randomly, if things look 'wrong'.

I have found Belbin's analysis very helpful when discussing the composition and balance of top teams, and commend it as a sound basis.[39]

Developing the Culture of Learning

To create effective organizations with competent directors it is necessary to have them operating on the higher plane of policy and strategy. But this plane is not about purely intellectual exercises which keep the directors' hands off the day-to-day operations of their business. Whilst thinking, and integrating the external and internal environments, are necessary functions of the business brain, there is a further process which needs creating and directing – culture.

The Cork Gully notion that 'mistakes are made because the climate for making mistakes exists' is a telling one. The converse is that directors can, and should, strive to create the organizational climate which avoids mistakes by encouraging learning. More specifically, directors have a duty to encourage a culture of learning throughout their organization and to manage the different layers of 'cultures' within their organization.

The commercial success of the book *In Search of Excellence*[40] did much to legitimize in a number of companies the idea that 'creating a culture of excellence' is a key directorial and managerial role. This is laudable. But the perspective on culture given in the book is essentially two-dimensional – which may help to account for the failure rates and problems of some of the selected 'excellent' companies.

I have written elsewhere of culture and the role of directors[41] and intend here to deal with just two points: what is meant by 'culture', and the four levels of culture.

I take 'culture' to mean the historically transmitted beliefs, behaviour, symbols and values of an organization. It is in essence the 'webs of signification'[42] we spin for ourselves via the symbols and practices and into which we often unconsciously and uncritically lock ourselves. Once in, it is hard to escape, but accepting the situation decreases dramatically the ability to learn and adapt.

Sir Winston Churchill, when planning the rebuilding of the House of Commons at the end of the Second World War, consciously allowed insufficient space for all members to have a seat easily. When questioned about such an apparently parsimonious approach, he explained that cost had not driven him at all. He wanted to ensure two things. First, that it would be difficult physically for cabals to form and stake out their territory. Second, that the random order of entry to the crowded Chamber would allow serendipity to operate, or at least force opponents to acknowledge each other.

His was a social/emotional approach, a subtle blend of Brownian motion and low cunning, which addressed the issue of creating debate. He was highly aware that the symbols we design and use, with architecture at the apex of the artefact design process, determine for a long time 'how things get done around here'. He was specific. He wrote, 'First we shape our buildings, then they shape us'.

I think that culture does the same. The blending of physical form, values expressed through rhetoric, and 'right and wrong' behaviour are all symbols of an organization's fundamental beliefs and aspirations. The director's role in this is to create cultures in which such symbols are positive and enabling rather than negative and blocking. The directors can, and must, design the heart of the organization.

This would assume a visual literacy as well as an intellectual rigour, and the ability to tolerate subordinates making mistakes provided they learn. All of these attributes can be learned by directors. The process is relatively easy to develop and can be highly enjoyable, especially if undertaken as a team development activity. It does have a profound effect on what people will and will not do in organizations.

There is a hierarchy of cultures to be managed by the directors too.

Level 4   *Meta* (integrating) cultures

Level 3   *Mega* (national) cultures

Level 2   *Micro* (organizational) cultures

Level 1   *Tribal* (specialist) cultures

The hierarchy of cultures in an organization

At the lowest level there are the 'tribal cultures' of the specialist functions and departments. Each has developed its own drama, rituals and routines. Each has its own initiation rites, taboos, and folklore. Each will try to exclude others if possible. Hence it is helpful for a director to have to work across specialist disciplines, to manage the boundaries, so that co-operation with, and valuing the work of, others is seen in the context of their contribution to the whole system, for if one person does not care, it can affect the whole. That may sound theoretical. But in practice if the last person to touch your product, the dispatcher on the loading bay, drops it and still sticks it on the truck, then no matter how brilliant the design and manufacturing system, you are still going to have dissatisfied customers.

Experiments and Action

The next level, the organizational 'micro-culture', takes a little longer to understand. There are various ways of describing the climate, or total culture, of an organization. Happily there are some excellent questionnaires for helping determine it. Here I will give you just one, powerful, model to demonstrate the process.

Charles Handy in *The Gods of Management*[43] builds on work which he and Roger Harrison have developed. He describes four main organizational cultures which, he argues, need careful identification before any organizational changes can be made to stick. He characterizes them as follows (but I must stress that the paraphrases are mine):

The Power Culture

symbol:

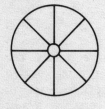

– very much the one-man-rule, or divide-and-rule, culture. Information is kept at the centre so that people operating on the spokes can be played off one against the other. Coalitions which challenge the centre are rapidly and ruthlessly put down. Such a culture tends towards win/lose fights and binary thinking. Little useful learning is possible for the majority but the folklore is rich in examples of the charismatic eccentricities of the person at the centre.

The Role Culture

symbol:

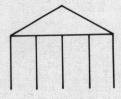

– essentially the bureaucratic model. Organizational procedures and values are highly codified and diffused. The people at the top are guardians of the status quo and tend to introversion and nit-picking. Everyone knows their place and there are tough sanctions should they step out of line. Making mistakes, or debating, is not encouraged and the folklore has horror stories about what happened to those who did.

The Task Culture

symbol:

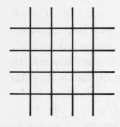

– essentially a project-based model. Teams are brought together for periods of intense work, then disbanded. There is a lot of energy around and people are usually respected for their contributions – everyone is working to time and cost constraints and appreciates their role in the project. Organizationally it can seem messy and there are great fights over who has the 'ultimate' power over a specialist, the project manager, or the head of the specialist function. Development can, therefore, be forgotten in the heady, action-based atmosphere unless ideas like 'centres of excellence' are introduced as counterweights.

The People Culture

symbol:

– an apparently 'anarchic' model in organizational terms. It is without government in the sense that the people in it subscribe to highly specific, and exclusive, values. The focus is on each person being treated equally, often as co-operators, with a say in objectives, product, and process. Whilst great fun to be in at the start-up, people cultures tend to hit trouble when faced with decisions on resource allocation and, sadly, become battlegrounds for interpersonal fights. Then little learning is possible and they tend to die rapidly.

Such an analysis can often help clear the directors' thinking. There are few examples of such 'pure' cultures. Most of us live in organizations which espouse one set of values but behave according to another. The very complexity of overlying levels of micro-culture is why directors need to spend time in clarifying the issues without losing the valuable differences found there.

The third level deals with national cultures, or 'mega-cultures'. I intend to say only a little on this here. It has been dealt with in a fascinating series of continuing research studies.[44] What I will say is that as trade becomes increasingly international, despite the efforts of the protectionists, the ability to cross national cultures in an effective way is becoming a major concern of directors. 'Technology transfer' often proves hollow if the transferee is neither historically nor culturally prepared to accept what is offered. Neither is the transferer usually prepared to spend time comprehending both histories and cultures to allow a bridge to be built rapidly between the learning systems of both. Hence we have problems when a UK company tries to acquire a company in such an apparently similar culture as the US; and we see major problems when, say, a French company tries to transfer high technology to Iraq or China. I believe that it is at this level that the *In Search of Excellence* thesis is faulty. Perhaps this fault is partly explained by research which shows the US as one of the two national cultures (the other is Japan) least able to adapt to, or value, others' culture.

Coming to grips with the mega-culture level can be an enlightening and enlivening experience for directors as it changes their perspectives radically. There are processes for helping here and the work of the Institute for Research into Intercultural Co-operation in Arnhem[45] deserves a special mention for its innovative work.

I argue that there must be a fourth level of culture, the 'meta-culture', which transcends and integrates the lower three. I would maintain that ultimately directors will have to strive to become meta-cultural managers. But for the moment that seems a long way off. In the meantime directors can concentrate on developing the cultures of levels one, two, and three so that learning predominates within their business.

Development Processes for Directors

I know that 'when there are alligators snapping at your tail it is difficult to remember that the problem is to drain the swamp'. But I do not accept this as an excuse worthy of a director. What are they doing in the swamp in the first place? They have staff employed to work there. I do accept, however, that carving out time to allow for the personal, professional and team development of directors is a difficult issue. It does not feel 'legitimate' somehow. Career paths usually stop short of director development and even a semi-public display of ignorance and/or lack of skills can discomfort many directors.

This latter objection can be dealt with in two relatively simple ways. First, development work for the team and the business can be done in short bursts off-site and combined with an action learning process which allows simultaneous personal and organizational development. Second, a lot of personal development can be done away from work altogether.

In my view there are three distinct phases necessary to allow directors to become comfortable with their roles in a learning organization.

First, there is a need to help people to let go of their specialist roles and come to accept the need to look upwards and outwards before integrating the whole. This is a psychological process of moving from a 'helpless' to an 'enabling' position – from reactivity to proactivity. This means moving from a position where directors feel they are on the receiving end of industrial, national, and global disruptions – and can do nothing about it – to a position where they are aware of the impact of environmental changes, have thought them through previously, and can reposition their organization to ensure continuing survival and growth.

To achieve this it is necessary for a director to be able to have time to think and learn the new role. It requires support from the top, and from colleagues. It is, therefore, often achieved most effectively as part of a top team development activity. As these psychological processes are well publicized I will not go into them in detail here.

The second phase is to rise above the 'normal' control systems of the business and create ones which give a true overview of the performance within and outside the business. To develop this structure so that it incorporates the ideas of synergy, system, and integration, it is necessary to look for ways of describing the performance of one specialist part of the business in terms of other parts, and the whole. The idea of describing output in terms of integrated statements, or ratios, allows both the quantification and quality of performance to be assessed. At present such statements are usually found in 'key ratios' which have been developed in various businesses and form the basis of directors' control information systems.

The very idea of running a business through the careful monitoring of a few key ratios seems curiously abhorrent to many directors. They complain that they need the fine detail to be able really to understand what is happening. The nature of director control is that you do not know the fine detail but, much more importantly, spend time looking at the broader trends which describe the way in which your operational learning loop is responding to your external environment learning loop via the integration of the brain of the firm.

An example of key ratios can be found in the process used by the General Electric Company of the United Kingdom. Many hold this to be a model of an effectively managed business. With 180 companies internationally, and a wide diversity of products and markets, it is noticeable that the key ratios developed by the managing director, Lord Weinstock, from the late 1960s still provide a sound basis for reliable assessment and debate between the individual business units and the corporate centre.

The key ratios are compiled monthly and measure the following variables:

1. $\dfrac{\text{Profit}}{\text{Sales}}$ %

2. $\dfrac{\text{Sales}}{\text{Capital Employed}}$ %

3. $\dfrac{\text{Profit}}{\text{Capital Employed}}$ %

4. $\dfrac{\text{Sales}}{\text{Inventories}}$

5. <u>Sales</u>
   Debtors

6. <u>Sales</u>
   No of Employees

7. Sales per £/$ of emoluments

Less effective companies often ascribe almost magical properties to the GEC ratios. There are none. It is a case of having selected helpful ratios for what the business considers important, then having the rigour to apply them and learn from them. Asking discriminating (some would say awkward) questions of his managing directors and top teams is the essence of Lord Weinstock's debating style. It is said to be rather intimidating when first encountered. I would argue that this is bound to be so, until the directors let go of the fine detail, whilst still being responsible for it, and start to manage the trends. They need to be fully informed but do not need to do the detailed work themselves.

GEC changes as the world moves on. The original seven ratios and monthly report and debate sessions have been adapted. The reports now include twelve 'salient figures' which record trends so that the seven ratios are seen in a wider perspective. The figures are submitted monthly but the debate is every three to six months at headquarters. The salient figures are:

1. Sales (£/$)

2. Orders received

3. Orders in hand

4. Net profit

5. Direct wages

6. Overhead spend

7. Capital employed

8. Stock

9. Trade debtors

10. Number of employees – direct
    – indirect

11. Average wage per hour of direct labour
    – basic rates
    – including premium payments

12. Export sales (from total sales)

This system has proved highly robust over two decades. It is not perfect; it places heavy emphasis on the operational/strategy spheres and less on the external environment. People learn that the figures can be adjusted in the short term, but this will reflect in the medium- to long-term trends so there is little advantage in so doing if they wish to have a career with the company. It is a practical example of the way key ratios can be derived to allow directors to transcend their specialisms and concentrate their energies on the interconnections between the specialist functions.[46]

The third phase of development is to get the top team into full debating mode. A little psychological help is often needed to ease the transition from monitoring the key ratios as a necessary but not sufficient part of the business towards having time to think and design the future. This latter includes having time to travel, read, and learn as legitimate direction-giving activities. This can cause some argument when put in such a bald manner.

I have found a helpful metaphor to be that of the relationship between an airliner captain and the aircraft's inertial guidance system. The intricate mechanisms of gyroscopes, feedback loops, and electronic processors takes careful constructing and installing. Once installed and tested it can be relied upon only if it is properly maintained (nurtured). The real problem is not the gyroscopic mechanisms but the discriminating questions that must be asked by the pilot – where are we going? what am I to do there? when? for how long? at what cost? etc. The flight crew (top team), cabin crew (the workforce), and the aircraft (organizational system) are the given boundaries of the problem. The trick is to steer the aircraft through many, often turbulent, environments to achieve the desired destination within the given constraints.

For a great deal of the time the aircraft can be left safely on automatic pilot. The operational system is self-correcting which leaves the captain time to monitor, and time to think. He or she can concentrate on the quality of the journey, and the service to customers, unless something exceptional happens when rapid actions must be taken. Through radar and radio there is a well-developed system monitoring changes in the external environment so trouble can be avoided. At intermediate points on the ground there are excellent maintenance facilities to ensure all machinery runs smoothly. One knows from airline research that the biggest problem of a well-run airliner is boredom. Once it sets in the captain may begin to test his limits, particularly by intervening in the operational cycle, to 'stretch' himself – to test just what he can do. We know that many crashes are caused in this way.

One can take metaphors too far. I realize that few organizational captains feel that they can sit back after take-off and trust their staff to get on with it whilst they adopt a management-by-exception stance. They could do it, but feel they should not. Even so, with the new computer capacity being installed in organizations it is relatively easy for directors to derive the necessary key ratios and still have time to think, provided only that they learn to delegate to and trust their staff. If a director can learn to do this, the problem is what to do then?

Sir Peter Parker when chairman of British Rail told of the positive responses from his senior functional colleagues (particularly those coping with the difficult industrial relations problems) when he delegated operational actions so that he could concentrate on the political and design aspects of the future shape of the railway. So much did his colleagues enjoy exercising their new responsibilities, their new rights and duties, that after a time they proposed a brief for their chairman which read as follows:

1. To keep out of the front line until they want me in – and then to get in there fully.

2. To resist getting into detail too soon; by keeping some distance I am in a better position to offer more objective advice.

3. To show consistency and steadfastness and to back them fully when the flak is flying.

4. To show understanding when people behave unpredictably, and when logic does not prevail.

5. To present our case powerfully to the outside world.

6. To ensure that, even in the heat of battle, I remind them of the long-term and social demands which must be tackled.

This seemed to be a useful confirmation of the notions I had been advocating. The latter point on long-term and social demands brings me back to the brain of the firm as the forum for organizational debate – the who? how? why? what? where? when? questions of policy and strategy. To achieve movement on this aspect there has to be both motivation and time, as I have already described.

Space Planning as a Tool

There is another issue, previously mentioned by Sir Winston Churchill, which needs consideration – space.

It is no coincidence that many of the companies which run into trouble have office designs which do not allow for directors' getting together on a variety of bases to debate. They may be physically separate, with their specialist function, and only come together as a whole for formal board meetings. They may be grouped in a long line along one corridor – the 'death row' of many companies – and hate it as they are neither with 'their' people nor able to work with other directors as a team. What seldom seems to happen is that space and/or process is provided for people to be able to integrate their work into the wider perspective. The parable of the blindfolded men trying to describe an elephant by touch often rings bells of recognition. It is significant that in areas of business where a director's personal fortune can hang on a colleague's decision, as in merchant banking, the partners share one space, often either side of one desk, so that all are aware of what is being done, on what information base, and on what terms.

Physical space is important to meeting and debating. If debating is going to be truly important for the organization the physical environment must symbolize that in this respect at least people are treated as equals.

Even something as mundane as the shape of the boardroom table can signify power and control in ways which are not appreciated or helpful. It is well known that the ideal shape for co-operation is the circle. How many boardroom tables do you know that are circular? If the table is oblong, then the position from which to chair a meeting is from the centre of one of the longer sides. How many chairmen do you know who chair from one end of the table and cannot, therefore, have easy contact with people at the far end of it?

If space is not easily available to allow all directors to work together, then the chance of meeting to kick around ideas and information semi-formally, or to gossip informally, should be encouraged. We know that companies rated as 'highly creative' by others tend to have elaborate eating and drinking rituals. We know that certain shapes will aid easy interaction. But if none of this works one can go off-site on a regular basis specifically to signify that this is out of the run of 'normal' work and is designed to encourage a more freewheeling and speculative form of thinking. The essence is to find time to debate, develop visions and ideas, hold back on evaluating those ideas too early, and get excited about what the future will be like if we design it our way.

Pulling this section together one can see a director's manifesto emerging for those organizations that will make it into the twenty-first century:

The Ten Necessary Characteristics of an Effective Director

1. I will play down my detailed, specialist function and learn to concentrate on managing the boundaries between my function and the others.

2. From this I will learn how to take an integrated overview of the performance of the total business, and my role in it.

3. I will learn how to delegate, and coach my staff, so that they can do the job for which they are paid.

123

4. I will give them 'cover' when necessary and will do this for the total organization when we deal with the external world.

5. I will broaden my horizons and role so that I become less political inside the business, and more politically aware outside it.

6. I will learn to become competent at exercising both the rights and duties of my directing role.

7. I realize that a balance has to be struck between achieving and nurturing and that it is my job to do this.

8. I realize that our organization is a part of our local and national society so I will try to take decisions which maintain and develop this relationship. We have rights and duties outside our own business to the communities which support us.

9. I will learn to design the future rather than just react to it.

10. I will be seen to have time to think in this organization.

The Contribution of Management Development to Director Development

Given the prejudices about each side, it is not surprising that directors and management developers, particularly 'trainers', rarely co-operate on director development. It is as difficult for a director to ask someone at a lower organizational level for help as it is for the developer to suggest that it might be needed and that he or she has something to offer.[47]

However, there is a wide range of processes available which can be brought to bear on the problem of director development. Britain is by far the most advanced country in 'distance learning', that is the transfer of educational information by post, radio, television, and telematic means. It has rarely been applied to director development but, in my experience, works well.

Before we go too deeply into the glories of interactivity, electronic bulletin boards, open-ended programming and other buzzwords that strike fear into the hearts of most directors, let us remember that we all have a large menu of management development dishes already available to us:

Newspapers and journals

Books

TV, films, video

Interactive videodiscs

Open courses – off site

Tailored courses – off-site

On-site courses

Self-development programmes

Distance learning systems – audio
                                                – televisual
                                                – written

Coaching and counselling

Job rotation

Secondments

Exchange programmes

The list is daunting but when one rises above the detail and reframes one can get a useful perspective.

The most important step in all this is for the chief executive and chairman to be seen publicly putting their personal commitment and financial support behind a director development programme. They must be committed to it. Mealy-mouthed support leading to an ineffectual programme can do enormous damage to a business in terms of the directors' loss of confidence in themselves, their value and competence. This has a severely damaging effect on some businesses, which takes years to put right.

'Legitimizing' director development programmes can be made manifest by giving each director an annual budget for their own development, and for the development of their people. This must not be controlled by the personnel function but must be seen as a line-management activity which will contribute directly to the effectiveness and efficiency of the business. Barry Welch of TSB Group suggests that there are four elements which can then help a director become comfortable with his or her role:

A personal development agenda

A director development agenda

A team development agenda

A business development agenda

One cannot tackle these simultaneously, at least at the start, nor need they be tackled sequentially, so let me explain each a little further.

The personal development agenda is to help with those aspects, often behavioural, which are seen as a block to career development. It may cover, for example, learning a foreign language, or golf, or learning how to entertain regularly both in restaurants and at home. It may also cover the perennial issues of personal health[48] and stress,[49] and the striking of a healthy balance between family and working life. Whatever the concern, the aim of the personal development agenda is to help release perceived personal blockages and deal with them in whatever manner the director feels most comfortable.

The director development agenda is to cope with 'all-those-technical-questions-you-have-always-wanted-to-ask-but-could-not-as-you-risked-looking-stupid'. Hopefully, this will avoid the Woody Allen problems with sex, and enable the director to become comfortable with the language, jargon, and thought processes of other specialist functions. Distance learning has been found helpful here. Managers learn well from audio tapes as theirs is a highly verbal culture. These can be used in the car to and from work, for example. Once tackled, the director development agenda can be highly liberating as it allows the setting of high professional standards.

The team development agenda is to help directors become part of the 'brain' function of the business, monitor the key ratios, loosen their grip on the details and so allow time to think, debate and design. Again, this can be a liberating activity for the top team provided only that the chairman and chief executive are totally committed to it. If not, it is wisest not to start.

The business development agenda is the final process of integrating the previous three agendas into the objectives of the business. As such it can be highly advantageous to use an Action Learning[50] process to achieve the necessary simultaneous developmental processes because it allows the specific issues facing a business at any one time to be addressed in a rigorous manner by the very people who will have to solve them anyway. It is a cost-effective form of development. An example of this is given in the case study beginning on page 129.

The idea of using development agendas is often greeted with a mixture of enthusiasm and scorn – because 'they would never let that happen here'. My response is that 'in the brain of the firm there are not many "they" and you are one of them!' So it is more a matter of getting agreement amongst yourselves to set aside time and money budgets for each individual, the top team, and the business; develop some assessment criteria by which to appraise the results; and get on with it. We are just starting such a process in a large financial services group and it has been received very well.

A more typical response by top managers to the issue of director development occurred when a memo was sent to all managing directors of an electronics group, which said that all MDs would attend a two-year Master of Business Administration programme. Just that. The result was to demean the notion that directors should continue to learn. So the very idea of director development was laughed out of court – to the dismay of many directors who had more modest but important agendas which were lost through the over-grandiose and thoughtlessly imposed plan.

The key issues for any development plan are that people are competent in their jobs, and that there is an effective and fair assessment system to ensure this. From these all else follows. This is as true of director development as any other. I have referred earlier to the characteristics I think are necessary for competent directors. The interplay between the personally-orientated learning cycle for personal and director development agendas and the organizationally-orientated learning cycle of the team and business development agendas can be shown using a double-loop learning

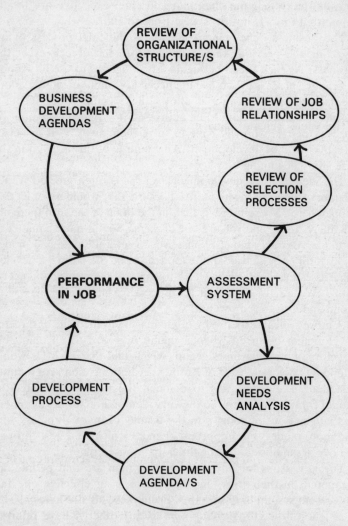

The double loop of personal and organizational development

model. In terms of development tools, this may be the best picture to hold in one's head when considering the development of directors (see illustration on previous page).

A Case Study: Round and Black Tyres

In 1977 I was asked to join as a consultant a seven-man top team which had been assembled to rescue the ailing truck tyre division of a major rubber manufacturer. The situation was officially 'desperate' and all directors knew that there was a maximum period of twelve months in which to turn the business round. After that, they had been told, their futures would depend on the impact they had made on profitability.

The young general manager, ably assisted by his management development adviser (who refused to act as 'just another trainer' and was an internal consultant throughout), looked at the mess and decided he had to rise above it and search for targets and key ratios which would allow the top team to begin to be able to measure their impact on the situation. He knew two key pieces of information. One, the market was going into a slump although, curiously, they were able still to sell all they made – the brand name was strong. Two, the Japanese were due to start landing truck tyres way below their company's cost price. These would start arriving within twelve months.

We did a quick and dirty 'team build' over a long weekend which mapped what resources we had to offer between us, discussed the differences, looked for gaps we needed to fill by using other staff (not by promoting them to director), and looked at where we had a surplus of strengths so that we could be aware where we might overdo things, whilst feeling very comfortable about so doing.

The top team did a detailed analysis of previous and projected figures and decided that there were two key objectives to reach by the end of twelve months:

1. Reduce the workforce by 50 per cent and improve the material flow to effect 40 per cent reduction in total factory/production cost.

2. Improve product quality by reducing warranty concessions by 20 per cent and increasing volume (the market liked the product when it could get it, even in a slump).

The numbers suggested that this would solve matters, but we all looked at each other rather bemusedly and asked, 'How do we achieve that?!' Then some reframing was done. Rather than say we had to do it, the question became how do we get our people to achieve that? This change of perspective was liberating as it allowed all sorts of ideas, and more doubts, to flow. The management development adviser reported that the shop floor was very interested in the new thinking which had been picked up rapidly on the grapevine, particularly as the directors were known not to be fire-proof and so were much closer to being 'one of us'. Meetings were laid on with union and staff representatives to explain the thinking so far. Tentative enthusiasm was expressed at these meetings but there was understandable concern about the possible job losses.

Whilst the functional directors worked as a team, together and apart, to sort out the logistics of reaching the two objectives, the general manager and management development adviser hatched a bold plan. They had doubts about the qualities of the middle management but realized that they would have to work with them. So they turned this to advantage by getting them into interdisciplinary groups of six people meeting regularly to look at the issues of cost/quality/people using a rigorous action learning process. Each group was to study the issue and implement actions to achieve the two objectives. They would report back to the top team on a monthly basis as a total programme so that they could play out a microcosm of the overall problem – actions taken in one area with a positive result often had a negative result in the other areas.

The effect on the middle management was galvanizing. They generated enthusiasm, rolled up their sleeves, spoke to other departments, argued, debated, and managed. This enthusiasm, despite the occasional bouts of depression and feeling of helplessness, was taken up on the shop floor where the workforce said they felt that for the first time in many years they had a management who were in the same boat as them and knew what they wanted. They developed their own mini-groups (remember that in 1950 the Japanese took action learning circles back to Japan and begat quality circles) on the shop floor. Other interesting things happened unexpectedly. The unions were officially against any job losses. Unofficially the local union representatives backed what was happening and helped with the reduction of the work-force numbers. This was achieved partly by their working cooperatively on the rules and benefits for early retirements, and redeployments, allowing for 'natural wastage', and partly by taking their own internal actions privately from management. It was noticeable that one Monday morning, without warning, there was a significant reduction in the head count. It later transpired that virtually all those with two jobs (one unofficial, like mini-cabbing) had had it suggested to them by the workforce that it would not be wise to show up on-site again.

The directors were greatly cheered by this help but still showed an alarming tendency to intervene in the middle management decisions if a chance occurred. The general manager and I worked on a second phase of director development which took them off-site regularly for a day where we debated what was happening on-site in key ratio terms, what actions needed to be taken to keep on track, and what was going on in the wider world. In the early stages, time was set aside to read newspapers and articles provided that people would then talk about the meaning of any topic in relation to the business. All of this happened at a golf club and the promise was that they would get a round in before dinner. They never did – everyone kept talking as they had a lot to learn and very little time to learn it. The process was not smooth and easy – this is a sanitized and simplified account – but the company did achieve the two objectives. Within a year they had moved significantly towards eliminating the losses and profits flowed by the end of the second year.

The irony was that by then the whole group was in deeper trouble. So what did the group do to their newly profitable busi-ness? They sold it to the Japanese! The lesson learned by the young top team was that enabling directors to think so that their organization can learn needs to affect the very top before it will ever be properly rooted.

Section Two
Some Possible Consequences

My work continues in this area so this is very much an interim report. However, it does seem that the ideas and processes for director development I have described do have liberating and energizing effects on organizations at all levels. Precisely why this is so I am not sure. I hope that academics will help with detailed research to specify and codify what happens so that we can use it widely. However, I am aware of four distinctly liberating aspects about which I will say a few last words.

First, clearing the hierarchy of policy/strategy/operations in a business and spending time getting the directors into their proper role gives both order and flexibility. It lets everyone know their place, their rights, and duties. It also allows a quality of thinking which can more easily cope with the ambiguity and uncertainty of the modern world, and can help directors value ideas and differences when related to organizational issues.

There is still a desperate search for certainty in many organizations, which saps energy and stifles enthusiasm. This is in part due to management educators still trying to stake a claim to traditional academic respectability and so teaching strongly along analysis-paralysis lines. What is ironic to me is that the very disciplines such academics would most like to emulate, such as mathematics and physics, have learned to take uncertainty in their stride. Since the 1920s Godel's theorem and Heisenberg's uncertainty principle have demonstrated that the only thing of which one can be certain is that you are uncertain.

Second, by clarifying roles one can get at such key organizational issues as control and ownership. The learning organization model demonstrates clearly where responsibilities, rights, and duties rest in an organization and where the boundaries are that need managing. At the director level I find that there is usually little doubt as to who is in control of operations – they are. But in terms of direction-giving, one comes back to the political world within which group boards, presidents, group chairmen, the shareholders, the bankers, pressure groups, etc. all have their say. Two phenomena strike me when I talk with people about this area. Using the learning organization process, the members of a company become more committed to it and its objectives. This can help reframe the problem of 'participation' in the organization. My dictionary defines participation as 'joint ownership and joint responsibility'. A lot of the union/management battles I have seen concerned the fact that the managers wanted joint responsibility without joint ownership, whilst the unions were pushing for joint ownership without joint responsibility. The learning organization seems to help strike a better balance between these.

Curiously, though, such clarification can expose directors to some harsh facts. It is unusual for them to own a significant slice of the equity of their business, despite stock options schemes etc. They are primarily agents of the shareholders and this can prove psychologically difficult over time. One highly successful managing director, headhunted every three years for increasingly complex assignments, put it simply: 'I am beginning to resent always being some anonymous shareholder's hit man. I know I do a good job, I know I leave behind healthy organizations, but I really am beginning to hanker after something I own. It's a deep psychological need.' Establishing a learning organization can expose such needs and pose discriminating questions over the psychological and financial ownership of organizations. It is up to us to deal with these creatively.

Third, using the learning organization process attacks the issues of organizational efficiency and effectiveness simultaneously. Efficiency comes from people in the organization's operational cycle having appropriate authority and responsibility delegated to them so that they have the commitment and discretion to do their jobs well. They can take a pride in being efficient, and then do not resent the challenge of being stretched by high targets – provided the top managers put enough nurturing into the system to ensure the necessary social/emotional lubrication. Effectiveness comes from the directors putting time aside to do a decent job of monitoring the external environment, debating issues and re-framing them. In this way the organization is always attuned to social, technological, and economic changes, which leaves it freer to design its future.

Fourth, and most important of all, the use of the learning organization processes generates healthier and more cheerful organizations. As the brain of the firm is developed, so organizations can begin to concentrate on their firm's heart. People can get enthused, and the dread Kafkaesque stereotypes of organizations dispelled. The unthinking use of military and bureaucratic language and images in organizations can lead to awful consequences and must be opposed at all times by directors. Organizations can lead to the greater benefit of mankind but, more typically, lead the people in them to feelings of powerlessness and pointlessness. I am reminded of David Lloyd George, Prime Minister, writing of the Flanders operation of 1917: 'For the massacre of brave men, who won just four miles of indefensible mud, the Government were not prepared by any warning or prediction given us by the military leaders. The full British casualties on the whole British front during the progress of the battle amounted to the appalling figure of 399,000 men – three times the official military estimate. Divisions were sent in time after time to face the same slaughter in their ranks. And they always did their intrepid best to obey the fatuous orders.'

Such lack of thought, and lack of information systems, are dangerous in any organization. In this case they devastated a continent. It can be argued that the scale of losses of population in such thoughtless battles explains the continuing decline of Europe during the twentieth century. The social and economic bases were eroded, never to recover fully.

It is against such horrors in organizational life that I am fighting. People will work cheerfully if they know what to do, have the tools and responsibilities to do it, get a just reward financially and psychologically for their work, and respect the directors for their proven direction-giving abilities.

That is the challenge I see for directors!

Notes

First a word of advice – this book should be considered in relation to two others: *Corporate Governance* by R. I. Tricker, Gower, London 1984; and a forthcoming book in this Fontana series, entitled *Information and Organizations*, by Max Boisot, Fontana, London 1987.

These both deal with new thinking on the role of directors and the design of organizational structures and processes, and will repay reading before setting out on the processes recommended here.

Preface

1. The GEC Developing Senior Managers Programme was written up in *More Than Management Development*, eds David Casey and David Pearce, Gower, London, 1977.

Part One – Reflections and Concepts

2. I was influenced by following the work of Peter Smith. His recent work can be found in 'The Stages of a Manager's Job', published in *Current Research in Management*, ed. Valerie Hammond, Frances Pinter Publishers, London, 1986.

3. Recent work on the formal roles of directors has been published in *Company Directors: their duties and responsibilities under the Companies Act 1985*, Hacker Young and Co., 2 Fore Street, London EC2Y 5DH, 1986.

4. The definitive work on action learning is R. W. Revans, *The Origins and Growth of Action Learning*, Chartwell-Bratt, Bromley & Lund, 1982.

5. Center For Creative Leadership, 5000 Laurinda Drive, Greensboro, North Carolina NC 27402, USA. Interesting work is being developed in this area by Professor Andrew Kakabadse at the Cranfield School of Management, Cranfield Insitute of Technology, Cranfield, Bedfordshire, UK.

6. Tom Wolfe, *From Bauhaus to Our House*, Abacus, London, 1983.

7. Alistair Mant, *The Leaders We Deserve*, Martin Robertson, Oxford, 1983.

8. Fontana, London, 1986.

9. Ashby's work was developed for Open Systems Thinking. I have taken the liberty of adapting its context. For its original presentation see, for example, W. R. Ashby, 'Self-regulation and Requisite Variety' in *Introduction to Cybernetics*, Wiley, London, 1956.

10. The operational side of making changes is dealt with competently in Roger Plant, *Managing Change and Making It Stick*, Fontana, London, 1987.

11. P. Watzlawick, J. Weakland and R. Fisch, *Change: Problem Formulation and Problem Resolution*, W. W. Norton and Co., New York, 1974.

12. Action Learning Trust, Luton, 1977.

13. See, for example, 'Managing Our Way to Economic Decline', R. L. Hayes and W. J. Abernethy, July/August 1980.

14. I. Ansoff, R. P. Declerck and R. L. Hayes, *From Strategic Planning to Strategic Management*, Wiley, London, 1976.

15. John Morris does not write enough! Unfortunately, I cannot refer to any written work by him in this area as I am assured there is none. He can be contacted at the Manchester Business School.

16. Donald Schon, *Beyond the Stable State*, Penguin, Harmansworth, 1967.

17. Alvin Toffler, *Future Shock*, Pan Books, London, 1981.

18. J. Naisbitt, *Megatrends*, Pan Books, London, 1983.

19. Peter Drucker, *The Age of Discontinuity*, Harper and Row, New York, 1968.

20. *Oxford English Dictionary*, Oxford University Press, London.

21. Tony Hodgson has not published in this area but his consultancy can be contacted at: Ellingstring, Nr Ripon, North Yorkshire, UK.

22. Allen Lane, London, 1972. As well as *The Brain of the Firm*, two later books by Stafford Beer should be noted: *The Heart of the Enterprise*, Wiley, London, 1979, and *Diagnosing the System for Organizations*, Wiley, London, 1985.

23. Joseph Heller, *Catch-22*, Corgi Books, London, 1964.

Part Two – Experiments and Action

The definitive reference work which no director should be without when entering these regions is: Charles Handy, *Understanding Organizations*, 3rd edition, Penguin Books, London, 1985.

24. D. A. Kolb *et al.*, *Organizational Psychology*, 3rd edition, Prentice-Hall, Englewood Cliffs, New Jersey, 1979.

25. A British version of the Kolb learning cycle is being developed, together with a database for comparison: Alan Mumford and Peter Honey, *The Manual of Learning Styles*, Ardingly House, 10 Linden Avenue, Maidenhead, Berkshire SL6 6H, UK., 1982.

26. Max Boisot's work, *Information and Organizations*, will be published by Fontana in November 1987.

27. See, for example, the issues raised for directors and senior managers in Sally Garratt, *Manage Your Time*, Fontana, London, 1986.

28. Sage, California, 1980.

29. BBC Publications, London, 1976. See also Tony Buzan, *Use Your Memory*, BBC Publications, London, 1986.

30. This will be published in book form by Collins under the title *The Colours of Your Thinking* in 1988.

31. Simon Jenkins and Anne Sloman, *With Respect, Ambassador*, BBC Publications, London, 1985.

32. Jacqueline Wonder, *Whole Brain Thinking*, Morrow, New York, 1984.

33. W. R. Bion, 'Experiences in Groups', in *Human Relations*, I–IV, Tavistock Publications, London, 1948–51.

34. McGraw-Hill, New York, 1976.

35. This is not in published form but can be learned through dramatic presentation from the Cork Gully Players (*sic*) at 3 Noble Street, London EC2.

36. I. L. Janis, *Victims of Groupthink*, Harcourt Brace Jovanovich, London, 1972.

37. The development of more creative use of non-executive directors is being led by two bodies in the UK: The Institute of Directors, 116 Pall Mall, London SW1; The Confederation of British Industry, Centre Point, New Oxford Street, London WC1.

38. Heinemann, London, 1981.

39. This theme is taken up in detail in Colin Hastings, Peter Bixby and Rani Chaudhary-Lawton, *Superteams*, Fontana, London, 1986.

40. T. J. Peters and R. H. Waterman, *In Search of Excellence*, Harper and Row, New York, 1982.

41. 'The Cultural Context' in *Handbook of Management Development*, 2nd edition; ed. Alan Mumford, Gower, Aldershot, 1986.

42. C. Geertz, *Interpretation of Cultures*, Basic Books, New York, 1973.

43. Pan Books, London, 1985.

44. To Hofstede and Boisot should be added S. Gordon Redding, 'The Management Education of Orientals', in *Breaking Down Barriers*, eds B. Garratt and J. Stopford, Gower, London, 1980.

45. The address is: Institute for Intercultural Co-operation, Velperweg 95, NL-6824 HH Arnhem, The Netherlands.

46. To help in this area I recommend Ray Proctor, *Finance for the Perplexed Executive*, Fontana, London, 1986.

47. Before starting out on such analysis it is helpful to reflect on what has taken you this far. I recommend highly Dave Francis, *Managing Your Own Career*, Fontana, London, 1986.

48. I am hoping to commission Suzie Morel to write a book on executive health, to include physical and mental health, exercise, sport, diet, etc. which we are hoping to publish in the Fontana series in 1988.

49. See, for example, Sandra Horn, *Relaxation: Modern Techniques of Stress Management*, Thorsons, London, 1986.

50. For some feel of the action learning process see Bob Garratt, 'The Power of Action Learning', in *Action Learning In Practice*, ed. Mike Pedler, Gower, Aldershot, 1983.

General Index

Index

Authors Index

Fontana Paperbacks
Non-fiction

Fontana is a leading paperback publisher of non-fiction.
Below are some recent titles.

- ☐ All in a Day's Work *Danny Danziger* £3.50
- ☐ Policeman's Gazette *Harry Cole* £2.95
- ☐ The Caring Trap *Jenny Pulling* £2.95
- ☐ I Fly Out with Bright Feathers *Allegra Taylor* £3.95
- ☐ Managing Change and Making it Stick *Roger Plant* £3.50
- ☐ Staying Vegetarian *Lynne Alexander* £3.95
- ☐ The Aforesaid Child *Clare Sullivan* £2.95
- ☐ A Grain of Truth *Jack Webster* £2.95
- ☐ John Timpson's Early Morning Book
       John Timpson £3.95
- ☐ Negotiate to Close *Gary Karrass* £3.95
- ☐ Re-making Love *Barbara Ehrereich* £3.95
- ☐ Steve McQueen *Penina Spiegel* £3.95
- ☐ A Vet for All Seasons *Hugh Lasgarn* £2.95
- ☐ Holding the Reins *Juliet Solomon* £3.95
- ☐ Another Voice *Auberon Waugh* £3.95
- ☐ Beyond Fear *Dorothy Rowe* £4.95
- ☐ A Dictionary of Twentieth Century Quotations
       Nigel Rees £4.95
- ☐ Another Bloody Tour *Frances Edmonds* £2.50
- ☐ The Book of Literary Firsts *Nicholas Parsons* £3.95

You can buy Fontana paperbacks at your local bookshop or newsagent.
Or you can order them from Fontana Paperbacks, Cash Sales
Department, Box 29, Douglas, Isle of Man. Please send a cheque, postal
or money order (not currency) worth the purchase price plus 22p per book
for postage (maximum postage required is £3).

NAME (Block letters) _____

ADDRESS _____

_____

_____

While every effort is made to keep prices low, it is sometimes necessary to increase them at
short notice. Fontana Paperbacks reserve the right to show new retail prices on covers which
may differ from those previously advertised in the text or elsewhere.